REMARKS
ON THE
THEORY OF MORALS:

IN WHICH IS CONTAINED

AN EXAMINATION OF THE THEORETICAL PART

OF

Dr. PALEY's

"PRINCIPLES OF MORAL AND POLITICAL PHILOSOPHY."

By EDWARD PEARSON, B.D.

RECTOR OF REMPSTONE, NOTTINGHAMSHIRE.

"NON TAMEN, POST TOT AC TANTOS AUCTORES, PIGEBIT MEAM POSUISSE SENTENTIAM; NEQUE ENIM ME CUJUSQUAM SECTÆ, VELUT QUADAM SUPERSTITIONE IMBUTUS, ADDIXI."

Quintilian.

IPSWICH:

PRINTED AND SOLD BY M. JERMYN.

SOLD ALSO BY MESSRS. RIVINGTONS, ST. PAUL'S CHURCH-YARD, AND HATCHARD, PICCADILLY, LONDON; DEIGHTON, CAMBRIDGE; COOKE, OXFORD; TUPMAN, NOTTINGHAM; ADAMS, LOUGHBOROUGH; STEVENSON AND MATCHETT, NORWICH; AND LODER, WOODBRIDGE.

1800.

[*Price, in boards,* 5s.]

ADVERTISEMENT.

THE Remarks, which are here presented to the public, were made in the progress of a course of Lectures in Morality, delivered to the Students of a College in Cambridge, in which Dr. Paley's "Principles of Moral and Political Philosophy" was the text book; that being the work, in which the public examination on moral subjects for a Bachelor's degree was then conducted. I indulge the hope, that, in endeavouring to facilitate the acquisition of clear ideas

on

on those subjects, in doing which I pretend to no more than the merit of a pioneer, I shall not be suspected of wishing to detract from the well-earned fame of Dr. Paley, or of any other writer, on whom I have had occasion to animadvert.

It may be proper to mention, that the quotations from Dr. Paley's book are made from the 8th edition in 8vo. In the different editions, there are many verbal variations; but I am not aware, that there are any, which materially affect the sense.

Of a work like the present, which professes to open the way to a system, and of which, therefore, the parts are just, only as they contribute to the perfection of the whole, the reader, it is hoped,

hoped, will have the candour not to make up his mind, until he arrive at the end.

E. P.

Rempstone Parsonage,
May 1, 1799.

P. S. Since these Remarks were first made, and since they were written in their present form, I have had the satisfaction to find, that, in some instances, they are confirmed by their agreement with those of that very accurate thinker and writer, Mr. T. Ludlam. See a work, entitled, " Six Essays upon Theological, to which are added two upon Moral, subjects. By Thomas Ludlam, A. M. Rector of Foston, Leicestershire." I beg leave to recommend the serious perusal of this work, as also that of another, by the same
author,

author, entitled, " Four Essays," to all students, who wish to obtain clear ideas on Theological or Moral subjects, and more especially on the former, or to be convinced of the importance of obtaining them. I am persuaded, that, for this recommendation, I shall receive the thanks of all, who may attend to it. It appears from these works (for of their author I have no other knowledge) that Mr. T. Ludlam is a true disciple of that school, which boasts the names of Butler, Powell, Balguy, W. Ludlam, *and* Hey.

January 1, 1800.

The Reader is requested to correct the *errata* previously to his perusal of the Book.

CONTENTS.

CONTENTS.

	PAGE
Introduction	ix

CHAPTER I.
On the *foundation* of Virtue*..............1

CHAPTER II.
On the *rule* of Virtue....................33

CHAPTER III.
On the obligation to obtain the *knowledge* of Virtue...............87

CHAPTER IV.
On the *motive* to Virtue.................119

CHAPTER V.
On the *division* of Virtue...............191

Conclusion................................225

---

* Though the word *virtue* among us, like *virtus* among the Romans, is sometimes used in a more extensive sense than is here intended, it is scarcely necessary to say expressly, that, throughout these Remarks, I mean to speak of *moral* virtue.

ERRATA.

P. 4, l. 14, *for* fome *read* fome.

33, l. 12, *for* geneal *read* general.

69, l. 17, *for* enquire *read* inquire.

146, l. 19, *dele* comma *after* epic.

150, l. 17, *instead of a* femicolon *after* motives, *put a* comma.

213, l. 2, *in the Note, put a* comma *after* which.

INTRODUCTION.

To those, who are beginning their inquiries into Morality as a Science, it is matter of great perplexity to find such a diversity of opinions, in the different authors they consult, with respect to its *first principles*. The variety of notions to be met with, respecting the *foundation, rule, motive*, &c. of virtue, is almost equal to the number of those, who have written on the subject.

Of the ancients, some (particularly *Thales*) thought, that, in order to be virtuous, we must avoid doing any thing, which we should blame in others. This, if it be considered as the *foundation* of moral obligation, evidently supposes a moral sense; since, without the assistance of such a sense, we should be under great uncertainty as to what we did or ought to blame in others. Probably, however, it was intended rather as the *rule*, than as the *ground* of duty. As such, it is of unquestionable utility, and agrees, so far as it extends, with the noble rule of conduct prescribed by our Saviour; to which, however, as comprehending only the *negative* duties of doing no harm, it must be acknowledged to be greatly inferior.

Some made virtue to consist in *following nature*. This opinion, though it contains

contains nothing pernicious, when it is rightly underſtood, was yet very liable to be perverted; and it was, accordingly, frequently perverted to very bad purpoſes; many ſuppoſing, that they were acting virtuouſly, whatever courſe they purſued, if they could but alledge, in defence of their conduct, that they felt an *inclination* to purſue it. As we proceed, we ſhall probably have occaſion to conſider this opinion more at large; as well as ſome others, which have had an extenſive reception and influence. For the preſent, it may not be amiſs to mention, reſpecting it, that it has been explained and defended by Biſhop *Butler,* in his three excellent *Sermons on human nature.*

Epicurus held, that virtue conſiſts in that exerciſe of the affections, which enables

ables us to possess the most perfect *pleasure*. It is well known, that this opinion also has been abused to pernicious purposes. It admits, no doubt, of an interpretation, which leads only to good. If, when understood as *Epicurus* probably intended, it be liable to blame, it is rather because it confounds *virtue* with the *motive* to virtue, than that it countenances actions, which the most rigid moralist would not approve; for it is certain, that, if we so act as to secure our most *perfect pleasure*, or, in other words, our *happiness*, which, as we consist of mind and body, must comprehend *mental* as well as *corporeal* pleasure, we cannot do any thing wrong; since, if we did, our *conscience* (admitting that constituent part of our nature as a *fact*) would not fail to embitter our reflections, and disturb our peace.

Cicero

Cicero thought, that virtue confifted in a conformity to right reafon; or rather, that virtue and right reafon were the fame *.

Potamon and others, who, from their felecting what they approved among the opinions of each fect of Philofophers, and rejecting the reft, were called *Eclectics*, made virtue to confift in *benevolence*; an opinion, which, under various modifications, has fince been very frequently revived.

Among the moderns, Mr. *Hobbes*, adopting the opinion of the Epicureans, makes virtue to be founded in *felf-love*.

Lord

---

* "Ipfa virtus breviffime *recta ratio* dici poteft."
Tufcul. 4. 15.

Lord *Shaftesbury*, in his *Characteristics*, thinks, that it consists in a conformity of our affections with our natural sense of the sublime and beautiful in things, or with the moral objects of right and wrong.

Dr. *Samuel Clarke*, in his *Evidence of natural and revealed Religion*, says, the moral obligations arise from the eternal and necessary differences of things, antecedently to all positive institution, and to all expectation of reward or punishment.

Mr. *Wollaston*, author of the *Religion of Nature delineated*, was of opinion, that moral good and evil consists in a conformity or disagreement to truth; in treating every thing as being what it is.

Dr. *Brown*, author of *Essays on the Characteristics*, after examining and condemning the three last definitions of virtue, proposes his own thus, " Virtue is the conformity of our affections with the public good; or the voluntary production of the greatest happiness."

Mr. *Hutcheson*, in his *Inquiry into the Original of our ideas of Beauty and Virtue*, refers virtue to a *moral sense*.

Bishop *Butler* also, who, as I have already observed, is an advocate for the principle of *living according to nature*, supposes a moral sense, making *conscience* the judge whether we do live according to nature (the *whole* of our nature or constitution) or not.

Mr. *Hume* makes a sense of *utility* the
sole

sole criterion (if not the foundation) of virtue.

Dr. *Adam Smith*, in his *Theory of Moral Sentiments*, resolves moral obligation into *propriety*, arising from a fellow-feeling or sympathy.

Lastly, Dr. *Paley* defines virtue to be " the doing good to mankind, in obedience to the will of God, and for the sake of everlasting happiness."

I am not aiming at a complete enumeration of the different opinions concerning the nature and foundation of virtue, which may be met with:

> " Non ego cuncta meis amplecti versibus opto ;
> " Non mihi si linguæ centum sint, oraque centum,
> " Ferrea vox."

This specimen will give a sufficient idea of
the

the diverfity itfelf, and of the perplexity thence arifing to a young inquirer.

It may, perhaps, be faid, that, fince the writers on morality, however they may differ in theory, agree, for the moft part, in the rules of conduct, which they lay down, this diverfity is not very material to the interefts of virtue; that, with refpect to any particular action, there is feldom any difference in determining on its nature, though the *criterion*, to which different perfons refer it, be not the fame. Be this as it may, it is at leaft defirable, as matter of *fcience*, that the principles, on which the obligation to moral duties ftands, fhould be reduced to that certainty, of which, from their nature, they are capable. It is fatisfactory to the mind to know, on every fubject, how far its powers reach, and how long refearch may be

continued

continued with the probability of success. I am, indeed, far from thinking, with Mr. *Locke*, that morality is capable of *demonstration*; as, in the course of my Remarks, I shall have occasion to shew more particularly. I am of opinion, however, that the subject may be delivered from many embarrassments, under which it now labours, and which give to morality an appearance of uncertainty and instability, not necessarily belonging to it. To deliver it from these embarrassments, is what I have *aimed* at in the following Remarks. How far I have succeeded, it is the province of others to determine.

REMARKS

REMARKS

ON THE

THEORY OF MORALS.

CHAP. I.

ON THE *FOUNDATION* OF VIRTUE.

THE want of distinguishing properly between *virtue* itself, and the *motive* to virtue, is, if I mistake not, one great cause of the obscurity, in which the subject of morals has been involved. In order to remedy this, I shall consider these, as also the other parts of the subject, *separately*, and endeavour to give each its proper place.

A criterion, by which moral good and evil may be determined with certainty, has long been confidered as a *defideratum*. How far moralifts have been from attaining to it, appears from what is faid in the *Introduction*. To difcover how far fuch a criterion is in itfelf attainable, we muft confider what is the *foundation* of morality; what it is, which makes an action to be good or evil; for it is necef-fary, that the criterion, in order to admit of general application, be commenfurate with the effence of that, of which it is the criterion.

I am aware of the difficulty and danger of defining, and it is not without oft-refumed confideration, that I write, *Virtue is voluntary obedience to the will of God.*

Now

Now, if this be a just definition of virtue, it will immediately appear why no criterion of it, which is universally applicable, has been, or can be discovered. It must be evident, that though, by some one or other of the various methods afforded by reason and revelation, we can attain to a knowledge of the will of God, respecting almost any action, of which we may be called upon to judge; yet there is not any *one* rule, to which the will of God, respecting *every* conceivable action, can be reduced. For, though our Saviour says, that all the law and the prophets (all the duty of man) hang on the two commandments of love to God and love to mankind; which two, he also says, are *like* each other, and which, indeed, are reducible to the single principle of *love*; yet, if I mistake not, this has no reference to the duty of

man,

man, as an *obligatory rule of life*; but is meant to be descriptive of that state of mind, to which, by the exercise of virtue, it should be the aim of man to attain, and which, when attained to, would render an obligatory rule of life unnecessary. As love, in this sense, would secure a fulfilment of the law, (whether we understand, by the term, the law of nature, or the moral part of the Mosaic law) it would also supersede the law. Moralists, indeed, at least the moralists of modern days, have generally *begun* their inquiries with seeking for some principle as the foundation of moral obligation, intending, as it should seem, thence to deduce the desired criterion of virtue. That they have failed of success, is a fact sufficiently ascertained. The reason, why they have not been immediately sensible of their failure, seems to be, that they have imperceptibly

perceptibly departed from the investigation of the *foundation* of virtue, to that of the *criterion* or *rule*; and that each, finding some rule more general, in his opinion, than another, has adopted it as an *universal* one; and then, confounding the two objects of inquiry together, has concluded that *rule* to be also the *foundation* of virtue. Let us examine this, with respect to some of the definitions of virtue most generally received.

According to Mr. *Wollaston*, the celebrated author of the *Religion of Nature delineated*, virtue consists in a "conformity of our actions with truth; in treating every thing as being what it is." Now, however useful this may be as a rule of conduct, yet, as it does not extend to the ground of moral obligation, I cannot consider it as a just definition of virtue. If

it

it were shown, that truth is the invariable *test* of virtue, that every action conformable to truth is virtuous, it would not follow, that it is virtuous *because* it is conformable to truth; for, since virtue implies obligation, it would still remain to be shown, that there is an obligation to act in conformity to truth. In fact, this is the process, which Mr. *Wollaston* pursues, and which brings him, at length, to what I consider as the true ground of moral obligation to human beings. "As," says he, " the owning of things in all our conduct, to be as they are, is direct obedience; so the contrary, not to own things *to be* or to *have been*, that are or have been, or not to be what they are, is direct rebellion against him, who is the author of nature." Also, speaking of virtuous actions, according to *his* idea of virtue, he says, " to do this, therefore, must be

agreeable

agreeable to the will of God; and, if so, the contrary must be disagreeable to it; and, since there must be perfect rectitude in his will, certainly *wrong*". What is this but an endeavour to justify his definition, by showing, that the breach of the obligation defined by it is disobedience to the will of God, and making the will of God the ultimate criterion and foundation of virtue? Afterwards, he says expressly, that " the law of the author of nature is the great *law* of natural religion;" which I understand to mean, that the will of God is the law of virtue *.

---

* The title of Mr. *Wollaston*'s work is, *The Religion of Nature delineated;* of which (page 25,) he defends the propriety, by stating what he takes to be the true sense of the word *Religion*. But, though that sense of the word be defensible, it is not the generally received one. By *religion* we generally mean something, which has an immediate relation to *God*. It would be better, therefore, in order to keep the sciences distinct, to confine the subject

On the other hand, Dr. *Samuel Clarke*, if I mistake not, in making moral obligation to arise from the eternal and necessary differences of things, antecedently to all positive institution, and to all expectation of reward and punishment, goes further than we are concerned to go, and overshoots the bounds of the science. " These eternal and necessary differences of things," he affirms, " make it fit and reasonable

subject of *Natural Religion* to the *being and attributes of God;* to those notions of a Deity, which we are able to arrive at by reason or (as it is sometimes called) the light of nature. All the *duties* of man, whether to God, his neighbour, or himself, form the subject and come under the title of *Moral Philosophy*, of which, in fact, Mr. *Wollaston*'s work is a system. Since, however, according to my notion of moral obligation, the duties of man are to be deduced from the will of God, it must be acknowledged, that there is a very close *alliance* between religion and morality; or rather, that there can be no morality (properly speaking) without religion; and I have no objection to that class of moral duties, which are due more immediately to God, being called *religious* duties, so long as it is understood to be by way of *eminence* only.

reasonable for creatures so to act; they cause it to be their *duty*, or lay an *obligation* upon them, so to do; even separate from the consideration of these rules being the positive will or command of God; and also antecedent to any respect or regard, expectation or apprehension, of any particular private and personal advantage or disadvantage, reward or punishment, either present or future; annexed either by natural consequence, or by positive appointment, to the practising or neglecting of those rules." Now this, as I conceive, is calculated rather for an inquiry on what grounds some actions are virtuous, and others vicious, in the estimation of *God*, than on what grounds they are, or ought to be so, in the estimation of *men*; what is the foundation of virtue to God (if I may so speak) than what is the foundation of human virtue.

But

But with this a moralist has no concern. However curious it may be as a *metaphysical* inquiry, and with whatever propriety it may be discussed in treating on *natural religion*, it tends not to elucidate the principles of *morality*, nor to enforce its practice. In doing or forbearing any action, no one can be expected to consider, whether it be agreeable to the eternal and necessary differences of things; nor, if he did, would his consideration render his doing or forbearing more or less virtuous; unless (what perhaps is often the case) under the *name* of acting from this or the like supposed principle, he had really in his mind a reference to the divine will, and was endeavouring, by an adherence to his principle, to *obey God*.

Dr.

Dr. *Clarke**, however, like Mr. *Wollaston*, after having endeavoured to show, that moral obligations are incumbent on all rational beings, antecedently to the consideration of their being the will and command of God; yet thinks it necessary to go on to show, as what most effectually enforces them on our observance, that " they are also the express and unalterable will, command, and law of God to his creatures, which he cannot but expect should be observed by them, in obedience to his supreme authority." So that, though he does not make virtue to *consist* in obedience to the will of God, he establishes a connection between them, which,

---

* It better suiting my purpose to examine Mr. *Wollaston*'s principle first, I have not been careful to observe the order of time, in which he and Dr. *Clarke* published. Dr. *Clarke*'s work was first published (or, however, preached) in 1705; Mr. *Wollaston*'s in 1722.

which, in practice, may anſwer the ſame purpoſe, and keep God continually in our view.

Dr. *Paley* ſays, " Virtue is the doing good to mankind, in obedience to the will of God, and for the ſake of everlaſting happineſs." This definition, according to Dr. *Paley*'s explanation of it, comprehends the *ſubject*, the *rule*, and the *motive* of virtue; the ſubject being the *good of mankind*, the rule the *will of God*, and the motive *everlaſting happineſs*. As a definition of virtue, I cannot but think this liable to objection in all its parts. With reſpect to the *ſubject*, or that, about which virtue is employed, I contend, that it does not properly form a part of the definition of virtue. Let us firſt ſee what virtue itſelf is. It will then be time enough to determine what actions are

are virtuous, and what are otherwise. But, were it proper to include, in the definition of virtue, the particular actions, which are to be denominated virtuous, it would be necessary to denote them by a term, which comprehends them *all:* whereas, I further contend, that the term of "doing good to mankind," is altogether an insufficient one for that purpose. Many instances of actions might be given, many are given in Scripture, in which, at the time of action, no reference to the good of mankind is discoverable; but which, being done in known or supposed obedience to the will of God, were yet unquestionably acts of virtue. Dr. *Paley* himself acknowledges and adopts the common division of virtue (i. e. the *subject* of virtue) into duties towards *God,* duties towards *men,* duties towards *ourselves;* and it is not easy to see how, with any propriety,

propriety, these can be all comprehended under the term of "doing good to mankind."

With respect to the "will of God," I cannot, of course, object to its appearing in the definition; but I object to the place it holds there. I contend, that the will of God is more than the *rule* of virtue; that, to human beings, it is the *ground* and *foundation* of virtue. In fact, Dr. *Paley* soon quits it as a *rule*, substituting the principle of *general utility*, as expressive of it, in its stead; and he sometimes (through the force of truth, shall I say?) admits it as the *foundation*. In the beginning of Book V. he says expressly, "Every duty is a duty towards God, since it is his will, which *makes it a duty*." In the 9th chapter of Book I. also, he says, that "moral obligation depends

depends on the will of God;---that the meaſure of right and wrong is the will of God;---that moral rules are deduced from the divine will."

With reſpect to the *motive* to virtue, which, according to Dr. *Paley*, is "everlaſting happineſs," I object to this alſo as part of the definition of virtue. When we have ſeen what virtue is, let us proceed to conſider the reaſons, which ſhould urge us to practiſe it. It would be hard to deny the capacity of being virtuous to all thoſe, who have not attained to ſuch a belief of a life to come, as to influence their actions; the caſe, probably, of the moſt reſpectable part, if not the majority, of the ancient heathen world*. Yet,

were

---

* Let it be recollected, that the belief of the ſoul's exiſtence after death, did not always imply the belief of a future *retribution*.

were this clause admitted into the definition of virtue, this would be the evident consequence. For, even though they " did good to mankind," and did it " in obedience to the will of God," it follows, from this definition, that they could not be virtuous in doing so, unless they also had regard to " everlasting happiness *."

With respect to this clause, it may also be observed, that, if *everlasting* happiness be the proper motive of virtue, the Chapter on *temporal* happiness, with which Dr. *Paley* introduces his inquiry into the nature of virtue, however excellent in itself, has no relation to the subject, and is therefore misplaced.

I now

---

* The Sadducees among the Jews, and the Epicureans among the heathens, totally rejected the belief of a future state. Shall we therefore say, that no Sadducee or Epicurean ever did a virtuous action?

I now proceed in the attempt to justify my own definition of virtue. It must, in the first place, be observed, that it is the idea of virtue as applicable to human beings, which we wish to ascertain; and that these beings were made and are preserved by God. Now it seems evident, at first consideration, that the duty of all created beings must depend on something, which has reference to their peculiar nature and situation; and nothing strikes us so forcibly, in this view, as the relation, in which they stand towards their creator. God, in all the works of creation, must have had some *design,* or exercise of his will, respecting the part to be sustained by them. Under the implied condition, therefore, that this design would be answered, all beings, whether animate or inanimate, were created, and are still preserved. Put the case, that we were made

by

by a being, who was of a moral character something different from that, which we have every reason to attribute to God. Would our duty have been exactly the same as it is now? It appears evidently to me, that it would not; not only because, in consistency with such a supposition, our minds would have been differently formed, and therefore a different conduct would have *appeared* to us as our duty*; but because a different conduct would have been pleasing to such a being, and therefore the proper part and duty of his creatures. In that case also, the *motives* to action would have operated in a different way; since we could not expect rewards from such a being, but by a conduct different from that, which it is now necessary to pursue for that purpose. I do not

---

* See what is said of the *moral sense*, in Chap. II.

not say, that those, who have mistaken the *real* character of the Deity, and acted accordingly, are therefore excusable in acting wrong. This is a different case. They *may* be excusable; but their excuse depends on the *circumstances* of their particular situation. It is, then, the duty of all created beings, *as such*, to obey the will of their creator; and we need not, I think, proceed any further to be assured, that it is the duty of man, as a creature and dependent, to obey the will of God. The attempt to trace his obligation to virtue to any higher source is, if I mistake not, as unnecessary, as it would be in vain. Distinctions must be made, of course, according to the nature and capacities of the created beings. Of all created beings, with which we are here acquainted, man alone is endued with what can properly be called liberty

of

of action. Consequently, he only is capable of *voluntary* obedience. Irrational and even inanimate beings, in performing the several parts assigned to them, obey the will of God; but, as they do it by a law of their nature, from which they have not the liberty of departing, their obedience may be termed *necessary*. Rational beings, like brutes, may sometimes obey the will of God without intending or knowing it, and, consequently, without having the merit of virtue in doing so. This may be called *accidental* obedience. For the sake of clearness, let us state the several kinds of obedience to the divine will thus,

1. Necessary obedience to the will of God.
2. Voluntary obedience to the will of God.
3. Accidental obedience to the will of God.

The first is the virtue, if such it may be called, of the irrational part of the creation*. The second alone, which implies an obedience both *real* and *designed*, is human virtue. The third, though it should happen to denote the same external actions with the second, might yet be the reverse of virtue; and, under any circumstances, could be called virtue only in a *figurative* sense. When Abraham, in obedience to the command of God, was preparing to sacrifice his son, he performed an act of the strictest virtue. This was both an act of real obedience to the divine will, and was understood by Abraham to be so. When Nebuchadrezzar, armed with the sword of the Lord†, chastised the nations, which had incurred the divine

---

* " The winds and the sea obey him." Matt. viii. 27.
† Ezek. xxx.

vine displeasure, his achievements, in *him* the result of ambition, however conformable they might be to the will of God, and however glorious in the estimation of men, had no claim to the merit of *designed* obedience to the will of God, nor, consequently, to the praise of virtue. When the unjust judge, parabolically referred to by our Saviour*, decided the widow's cause, the action itself was one of those, which must ever be agreeable to the will of God; yet as, in performing it, the agent had no " regard to God," it was not in him an act of virtue. When the Jews persecuted the apostles of our Saviour, " *thinking* to do God service," they cannot be supposed to be even free from *guilt* in doing so, however their ignorance

---

* Luke xviii. It will be seen, that I make use of these instances from Scripture, not as *authorities*, but as *illustrations*.

ignorance of God's will might extenuate their guilt. When the Jewish rulers, in conformity with the "determinate counsel of God," crucified our Saviour; though they thus *accidentally* obeyed the will of God, their action was yet the very reverse of virtue, and deserving of the highest condemnation. For though, in this instance also, it be admitted, that they acted in *supposed* obedience to the will of God*; yet their action was not such as, independently of the great purpose intended to be answered by it, would have been *really* acceptable to God. It was one of those cases, and indeed the most eminent of all, in which the wisdom of God makes use of the wickedness

---

* See Acts iii. 17.

ness of men to effect his purposes of good*.

Concerning the virtue of respectable heathens, such as *Socrates, Plato, Cicero,* &c. we shall have occasion to speak more particularly in the Chapter on the *motive to virtue.* For the present, it may be sufficient to say, that the definition, which I have given of virtue, does not exclude any but Atheists from the ability of being virtuous. With respect to these, it is evident, that they cannot voluntarily obey the will of that Being, whose existence they deny. It happens, however, through the provident goodness of God, in making duty and immediate self-interest

to

---

* Acts ii. 23. I have elsewhere endeavoured to trace the progress to that state of mind, in which men do wrong on a right principle. See the 6th, 10th, and 12th of my "*Discourses to Academic Youth.*"

to agree in so many instances, that even Atheists may often *accidentally* obey the will of God, and thus perform the same actions, which a believer in God performs from a sense of duty.

Though the principle, which I have assigned as the foundation of moral obligation, be not recognised as such by the generality of moralists in *form*, it is so, if I mistake not, in *fact*. Were not this the case, I should be greatly apprehensive of its truth*; for I cannot easily persuade myself

---

* Let it be remembered, that the inquiry is not about the definition of the *term* virtue (for I consider not whether it be more properly called *virtue*, or *duty*, or *moral right*, or *moral good*), but about the definition of the *thing* intended by that term. The definition of a *term* can be only *improper* (unless it also imply an *affirmation* of its propriety) but the definition of a *thing*, professing to explain in what the nature of that thing consists, may be *false*. See *Watts' Logick*, Part I. Chap. 6. Sect. iv.

myself, nor can I hope to persuade others, that the true ground of moral obligation has been hitherto unknown or disregarded in practice, however it may have been obscured in theory. With respect to Dr. *Paley*, indeed, his definition does not *exclude* a reference to the divine will, though, as I think it ought, it be not simply confined to it; and I have already noticed, that he has, incidentally, referred to it as the *sole* ground of moral obligation. Mr. *Wollaston* and Dr. *Clarke* also, as we have seen, have, in some way or other, *combined* a regard to the will of God in every action, which they deem virtuous; though, as I think, not in perfect consistence with their respective systems. If acting in conformity to truth, or to the eternal differences of things, were the essence of virtue, there might be virtuous actions without any regard to the

Deity;

Deity; and the confideration of any notice, which he might be fuppofed to take of our actions, would come in only under the head of *motives*.

I may add, in confirmation of the notion I have adopted, that though, for reafons to be affigned hereafter, a fyftem of moral philofophy is not to be fought for in the Scriptures; yet it is not to be imagined, that they would refer to any other foundation of virtue than the true one; and certain it is, that the foundation, to which they conftantly do refer, is the *will of God.* " Keeping the commandments of God," " doing the will of God," " living to the will of God," " right in the fight of God," and expreffions of the like import, are thofe, by which the conduct, ufually denominated virtuous, is almoft invariably denoted. In the form of of prayer, which was given us by an infallible teacher, we are directed to pray for the general prevalence of virtue under the same idea; namely, that the will of God may be obeyed on earth, as it is obeyed in heaven. In short, I do not find in the Scriptures any general expression, under which virtue, as here meant, is comprehended, but *obedience to the will of God*; and I cannot think it safe to depart from the idea of virtue, to which the Scriptures constantly adhere.

On a subject of this nature, I can neither expect nor desire, that the opinion of any one should have weight, further than as it is supported by reasoning. It cannot, however, but be satisfactory to know, that the notion of moral obligation here asserted, is sanctioned by the opinion of of so accurate a thinker as Mr. *Locke*. In his Chapter of moral relations *(Essay,* Book II. Chap. 28.) he says, " The divine law, that law, which God has set to the actions of men, whether promulgated to them by the light of nature, or the voice of revelation, is the measure of *sin* and *duty*. That God has given a rule, whereby men should govern themselves, I think there is nobody so brutish as to deny. He has a right to do it; we are his creatures. He has goodness and wisdom to direct our actions to what is best; and he has power to enforce it by rewards and punishments, of infinite weight and duration, in another life; for nobody can take us out of his hands. This is the only true touch-stone of *moral rectitude*; and by comparing them to this law it is, that men judge of the most considerable *moral good* or *evil* of their actions; that is, is, whether as *duties*, or as *sins*, they are likely to procure them happiness or misery from the hands of the Almighty." Afterwards, indeed, he refers what *he* calls virtue and vice (or rather, what he says are so called by *others*), as distinguished from right and wrong, to the law of *opinion* or *reputation*; but it is evident, that he does not there mean virtue and vice in the sense, in which we are seeking for the foundation of them. What *Paley* and many other moralists intend by the terms *virtue* and *vice*, Mr. *Locke* has comprehended under those of *duties* and *sins*; so that, though there be an apparent opposition to the notion I have stated, there is a real and full agreement with it. With respect to the greater propriety of the terms *virtue* and *vice*, or *duties* and *sins*, it is hardly worth while to consider that question here. Yet we may observe,

in

in passing, that Mr. *Locke* (Book I. Chap. 3. Sect. xviii) thus recognises the sense of the word virtue, which later moralists have generally adopted: "If virtue be taken for actions conformable to God's will, or to the rule prescribed by God, which is the true and only measure of virtue, when virtue is used to signify what is in its own nature right and good; then, &c." though even there he contends, that virtue is more commonly understood to mean "those actions, which, according to the different opinions of different countries, are accounted laudable." But this, as I have said, is only a question about the propriety of the term, not about the truth of the thing.

I conclude, then, with repeating, that *Virtue is voluntary obedience to the will of God.* In other words, what God commands

commands is *right*, and right *because* he commands it: what God forbids, is *wrong*, and wrong *because* he forbids it.

CHAP.

CHAP. II.

ON THE *RULE* OF VIRTUE.

AFTER ascertaining the *foundation* of moral obligation, or what it is, that makes an action to be virtuous or the contrary, which, if I mistake not, we have seen to be the *will of God*; the next thing is to consider what is the *rule* of virtue, or what are the means, by which we may discover, in each particular case, what the will of God is.

Mr. *Wollaston* speaks of the " long and laborious inquiry, which has been made after some geneal *idea*, or some *rule*, by comparing actions with which, it might appear to which kind (good, evil, or indifferent) they refpectively belong;" and fays, that " though men have not yet agreed upon any one, yet one certainly there muft be." This he probably fays under the apprehenfion, that, if no fuch general rule exifted, virtue and vice would be things uncertain in their nature, and liable to vary with the varying opinions of men. As it refpects the *foundation* of virtue, this apprehenfion is juft; but not fo, I think, as it refpects the *rule*. If we have rightly fixed on a foundation, which is invariable, we need not be in fear, as to the *ftability* of virtue, for want of an univerfal rule. I have, therefore, no hefitation in faying, that if, independently of that, which *determines* the moral quality of actions, we feek for a rule, which may ferve as an infallible *teft, criterion,* or *touch-ftone* of virtue, we feek for that, which can never be found. If the

the rules of virtue, which have been fixed on by moralists, are not also the *foundation* of virtue, they cannot be expected to hold universally. No doubt, many rules of conduct, which have no immediate reference to the foundation of virtue, may be both safe and useful; but they must always be laid down under certain limitations, expressed or understood; nor do I see how any *one* rule, other than one of equivalent meaning with the foundation itself, can comprehend *all* the actions, which ought to be comprehended as virtuous, or, considered abstractedly, denote in *any* the quality, which alone renders them virtuous. No action can properly be called virtuous, which has not reference to that, which makes it so. If virtue be obedience to the will of God, I do not see how any action, which has not a reference to the will of God, can be considered fidered as virtuous; and, though many actions, which have not an *immediate* reference to the will of God, may be virtuous, yet they can be fo only in proportion as they are conformable to a rule, which is *fuppofed* to be expreffive of that will. To proceed by a rule of conduct, of whatever nature it may be, independently of its being confidered as a declaration of the will of God, is not, as I conceive, to act virtuoufly. In proportion, therefore, as any fuch rule carries off the mind from that, which is the conftituent of virtue, it ceafes to be a rule of virtue. If it were poffible to perfevere in a courfe of thofe actions, which are ufually called virtuous, merely becaufe they are conformable to truth, or to the eternal differences of things; becaufe they are conducive to the public good, are the dictates of reafon, or the fuggeftions of of the moral sense, or so on; without having any reference to their being also agreeable to the will of God, they would not, if my idea of virtue be the right one, be *virtuous* actions. It is not to me, therefore, a subject of regret, that no rule of this sort is found to extend to every conceivable action. Indeed, since such rules are useful to the purposes of virtue, only so far as they are intermediate steps to the knowledge of the divine will, the circumstance of their being universally applicable might be of dangerous tendency, and contribute to fix the mind on them as the ultimate object in view. Let us, however, examine some of the most celebrated of these rules, in respect both to their abstract signification, and as they are expressive of the will of God.

With respect to conformity to the eternal differences of things, or to truth, it is not easy to admit, that either, in itself, is an adequate criterion of virtue; since many actions may be conceived, which, though not conformable to either, would yet be no infringement of moral obligation. The ludicrous instance of " talking to a post, or otherwise treating it as if it were a man," which is mentioned by Mr. *Wollaston*, is of itself sufficient to show, that neither his rule, nor Dr. *Clarke*'s, are adapted, in all cases, to distinguish the moral qualities of actions. That action would certainly be a breach of both their rules: it would neither be conformable to the eternal differences of things; for it would be confounding things essentially different: nor would it be agreeable to truth; for it would not be treating a thing as being what it is: yet no one, I suppose,

suppose, would admit, that such an action is *morally* wrong. The proper rule of virtue, if I mistake not, would leave such an action as *indifferent*; that is, would not extend to it at all. On the other hand, there are, I conceive, many wrong actions, of which we cannot discern the incongruity with the eternal differences of things, nor with truth; and many virtuous ones, of which we cannot discern the agreement: at least, there are many cases, in which the application of either rule would be matter of greater difficulty than a direct reference to that, which I esteem as the foundation of virtue, and in which, therefore, no advantage would be gained.

It may perhaps be urged, that, since Dr. *Clarke* and Mr. *Wollaston* have deduced the most important moral duties

from

from their respective rules, those rules must at least be of equivalent meaning with that, which is the true criterion of virtue. It may be observed, however, that the very circumstance of both having deduced the same duties from different rules, affords a presumption, that neither of them has hit upon a rule, which is exclusively the right. I have, besides, already shown, that they have not done this without reference to something extraneous to their rules; and I now further contend, that, if they had, all that could thence be fairly concluded is, that the rules of both, so far as they are applicable, are *not inconsistent* with the true criterion of virtue; a conclusion, which I have no inclination to deny. Since God is the *author* of all things, and of their various relations and dependencies, and since he cannot be *contradictory* to himself

self, it is doubtless true, that both these rules are in *conformity* with his will; and the ingenuity of a *Clarke* or a *Wollaston* could, with almost equal ease, from any other extensive principle, which was only *not inconsistent* with his will, have deduced our obligation (I do not say how convincingly) to the observance of the same duties*.

The same may be said with respect to morality as known by the ancient heathens. It may be asked, 'If the will of God be the foundation of morality, how came it to pass, that morality was carried to such perfection by those, who, from their want of revelation, were so imperfectly acquainted with the will of God,

---

* "It is possible," says *Hooker*, " that, by long circumduction, from any *one* truth all truth may be inferred."

God, and who, in fact, so seldom referred to it?' In the first place, it is by no means to be admitted, notwithstanding the excellence of many ancient treatises on the subject, that morality *was* carried to any thing like perfection by the heathen philosophers. Certain at least it is, that some of the wisest among them, aware of their deficiency in this respect, confessed the want of further information than mere reason could afford. *Socrates*, or rather *Plato* under the character of *Socrates*, seems to have been sensible of the want of revelation, even for the purpose of teaching the duties of morality, when, after discoursing with *Alcibiades* on the difficulty of properly performing the duty of prayer, he said, " Αναγκαιον ꭒν εϛι περιμενειν εως αν τις μαθη ως δει προς θεꭒς και προς ανθρωπꭒς διακεισθαι : we must wait patiently, therefore, 'till some one

one shall instruct us how we ought to conduct ourselves towards the Gods and towards men;" which some have understood as predictive of our Saviour*. It is at least a confession, from one of the wisest of uninspired men (for such we must reckon either *Socrates* or *Plato*) that a revelation of the will of God was not an unnecessary thing, even in teaching us what our duty is†. Now it is the method of revelation, so far as it teaches us what our duty is, to declare and explain the *will of God*; for it is to the will of God, as I have already observed, that the Scriptures constantly refer, as the proper criterion

---

* See the substance of this *Dialogue* in No. 207 of the *Spectator*.

† The *great* object of revelation, however, at least according to the commonly received opinion, and as we shall have occasion to notice more particularly hereafter, is rather to furnish sufficient *motives* to right conduct, supposing it known, than to declare what right conduct is.

criterion of virtuous conduct. The Gospel in particular, that full revelation of the divine will, to which such well-disposed heathens may be considered as having looked forward, teaches us, that the greatest good, to which man can aspire, is a sense of the approbation of his maker; that this, in every stage of his existence, must be the foundation of his happiness, and the only unchangeable part of it; and that, in order to obtain this approbation, we must so conform our conduct to the will of God, as to be renewed to his image, in which we were originally made. Further, to render this an intelligible lesson to us, the veil, which intercepted our view of the Deity, is partly removed; and his attributes, so far as they can be the objects of our imitation, made visible to the human eye. And, doubtless, mankind stood greatly in need of such information.

mation. The *wisdom* and *power* of God, indeed, were so manifest from the works of creation, that the heathens could not well overlook them; but their idea of his *moral* attributes was so corrupt, that it ill deserved to be the pattern of imitation. The perfections of holiness, justice, and goodness, were sometimes entirely forgotten, sometimes the subject of dispute, and were scarcely ever admitted without a mixture of the opposite imperfections. We may allow, however, without danger of any ill consequence, that, in all the great points of conduct, the rules prescribed by the most esteemed of the heathen moralists are just. To such acute observers, as some of the ancient philosophers undoubtedly were, the contemplation of human life could not fail to point out that conduct as proper for man to pursue, which, tending to the happiness

of

of individuals, the prefervation of fociety, or fome other immediate good purpofe, was really, in all material inftances, conformable to the will of God, whether it was *confidered* as being fo, or not. But, though fuch rules of conduct had been in *exact* conformity with the will of God; yet, unlefs they had alfo been underftood and believed to be fo, they could not have claimed fubmiffion from the people. We find, accordingly, that the fpeculative opinions of philofophers had but little effect in regulating men's conduct. The depravity of the heathen world is well known, and need not be dwelt on here. St. *Paul*, in the firft Chapter of his Epiftle to the *Romans*, has given the ftriking outlines of the horrid picture. " Human nature, having acquired a bias towards fin, was verging to the extremes of impiety, oppreffion, and licentioufnefs.

The

The worship, due to the great Creator, was altogether withheld, or paid where it was not owing, and in a manner, which rendered it an abomination. The greater part of men, instead of endeavouring to promote universal happiness, by a due discharge of their relative duties, and by a care, that their own welfare should interfere as little as possible with that of others, suffered every consideration to give place to the desires, which views of immediate self-interest inspired. Instead of seeking, in the cultivation and amendment of their minds, the proper happiness of a rational creature, they sunk into brutal gratifications of sense, neglecting the superior parts of their nature, and grossly abusing the rest*." Even in the celebration

---

* See my *Essay on the goodness of God, as manifested in the mission of Jesus Christ*. In the course of my Remarks, I have

celebration of their solemn religious rites, they were often guilty of great impurities and cruelties; and it was well if, in their endeavours to recommend themselves to one or other of their Deities, by imitating the several qualities attributed to them, they did not transgress every rule of morality. I am, indeed, far from denying, that there was any virtue in the heathen world. Though the heathens were not so fully acquainted with the will of God as we are, nor so mindful of it in their conduct, as they might and ought to have been, they were not altogether ignorant of it, nor universally inattentive to it. I contend, however, that, in those instances, in which they did act virtuously, they had respect to something

independent

---

have made use of a few other ideas, contained in the same Essay, without a formal acknowledgment of having published them before.

independent of those rules of philosophy, which were made out on the principles of abstract reasoning. Whatever was the case of philosophers, in their speculations, the common people, in their practice, had a view to what they esteemed pleasing in the sight of God*. Else, what meaning was there in their expiatory sacrifices, and religious feasts? It was this, if I mistake not, which rendered that *virtue*, which otherwise had been only *prudence*†.

---

* It is thus, that common sense sometimes directs to truths, from which the too ardent pursuit of speculation leads astray. While philosophers were puzzling themselves and others with unsatisfactory, not to say inconsistent, schemes of morality, made out on abstract reasoning, the multitude looked immediately to God. Even the uninstructed *Indian*, his thoughts directed to the source of his existence,

"Sees *God* in clouds, and hears him in the wind."

† I do not distinguish virtue from prudence (taking the latter in the common acceptation) as Dr. *Paley* does, by a reference to *motives*, making them to differ only in *degree*; but by a reference to the *principle* of action, making

The principles, on which the morality of the multitude was founded, may be more truly traced in the writings of the *poets*, than in those of the *philosophers*. The poets are, at least, more exactly descriptive of real life; if they are not also those, who, according to *Horace's* character of the greatest among them,

"—quid sit pulchrum, quid turpe, quid utile, quid non,
"Plenius ac melius Chrysippo et Crantore dicunt."

And certain it is, that, with the poets, *obedience to the Gods*, such as their idea of obedience to the Gods was, is the principle of almost every virtue, by which the hero of Epic or Dramatic story is attempted to be exalted. I believe, in short, that many of the heathens, perhaps *all* of them at one time or other, did some things,

---

making them to be things *essentially* different. The reader will see my reason for doing so, when he comes to the Chapter on the *motive* to virtue.

things, and abstained from doing others, merely because they considered them as pleasing or displeasing to their Gods; and I conceive, that these, being at the same time actions or forbearances in themselves agreeable to the will of God, or at least not in opposition to it, were, under the circumstances, in which the heathens lived, so many instances of real virtue.

I contend, moreover, that even the philosophers, in their notions of morality, were not altogether inattentive to the will of God, as the principle of virtuous conduct. It is true, indeed, that those of them, who, from impatience of leaving any thing unsettled*, or the vanity of

being

---

* It is not in the instance of the *heathen* philosophers alone, that the want of the επεχειν, a state of mind so suitable to the nature and situation of man, has been productive of ill effects.

being at the head of a sect, attempted to form complete *systems* of morality, were sometimes led to leave this foundation, and to proceed on imaginations of their own. This, however, may be satisfactorily accounted for, without any presumption against the truth of what I have advanced. Though God never left himself without witness, being discoverable, in some degree, both in his nature and in his will respecting us, from his works of creation*; and though, from the contemplation of those works, as I have already admitted, some of the wisest among the heathens were able to deduce the most important moral duties; yet, whatever was the cause,

---

* *Cicero* says, " Credo deos immortales sparsisse animas in corpora humana, ut essent, qui terras tuerentur, quique, cælestium ordinem contemplantes, *imitarentur* eum vitæ modo atque constantiâ. Nec me solùm ratio ac disputatio impulit, ut ita crederem; sed nobilitas etiam summorum philosophorum et auctoritas.

cause, the knowledge of God's will was, in fact, so obscured, that, independently of assistance from revelation, men would in vain have attempted to build upon it a complete *system* of moral duties. Those, therefore, who aimed at forming a more extensive scheme of morality, than the state of their knowledge of the divine will enabled them to do with satisfaction to themselves, relinquishing what they considered as an insufficient guide, deduced men's duties from some abstract truth; often delivering, it must be owned, useful directions for the conduct of life, though from a principle exclusive of real virtue. Of this the *Offices* of *Cicero*, which, with respect to precepts, may be considered as the result of heathen investigations into the science of morality, are a striking instance. So far as they go, they rightly point out what our conduct

ought

ought to be; but they are silent about the principle, which alone can render it *virtuous* conduct. They are the *body* of virtue, if I may so speak, without the *soul**. This, however, was not the case of those among the heathen philosophers, who obtained the most esteem, and whose lessons had the most extensive influence. The early Grecian philosophers more especially, in effect, though not systematically, very frequently referred to the divine will as the proper rule of human action, not to say as the ground of moral obligation. *Plato*, we are expressly told †, maintained the opinion, that " the ultimate end of man consisted in obtaining a likeness to God;"
which

---

* I speak not here of their deficiency in respect to *motives*. That is a part of our subject, which will come to be considered hereafter.

† Diogenes Laertius, Lib. III. Segm. 78.

which certainly implied, that the will of God was the proper *rule* at least of human conduct, if not the ground of obligation to virtue; and we have already seen, that, under the character of the wisest of uninspired men, he was content, in one instance, to wait patiently for a fuller manifestation of the divine will, rather than proceed on uncertain speculation*. The *Memorabilia* of *Socrates*, as exhibited by *Xenophon*, will give ample testimony to the same truth, with respect to *Socrates* himself; who, indeed, conformably to the idea I am endeavouring to give of a virtuous man, seems, in the regulation of his conduct,

---

* Even *Cicero*, on some occasions, refers both the rule and the ground of duty to the divine will. See, particularly, his treatise *De. Leg.* 2. 4. also *Frag. de Repub.* 3. apud Lactant. 6. 8.

conduct, never to have suffered *God* to be out of his thoughts*.

Let us proceed to consider the principle of *general utility* as a criterion of virtue. This is the rule of virtue adopted by Dr. *Paley* †. For though, in his definition of virtue, he makes the *will of God* to be the rule of it, he afterwards,

as

---

* It may, perhaps, be said, that this is rather the character of a *religious*, than a *virtuous* man. I hope, however, that, on a little confideration, my notion of virtue will not therefore appear the less juft. There is, indeed, a *primâ facie* prefumption, that what is the foundation of virtue to a *religious* man, muft be the foundation of virtue to all other men; fince a religious man differs from others, who have any juft pretenfions to virtue, not in acting on a different principle, but in paying peculiar attention to that clafs of moral duties, which are owing more immediately to God, or which have God for their immediate object.

† Mr. *Hume* feems to go fo far, as to make utility the *ground* of virtue, which is fomething more than making it the *rule*: but I hope that, on this part of the fubject, enough has been faid in the firft Chapter.

as I have already observed, substitutes the principle of general utility as *expressive* of that will. I have already stated my reasons, why I do not admit a regard to utility to be the *ground* and *foundation* of virtue; that is, why an action is not *therefore* virtuous, *because* it tends to the good of mankind. I have now only to consider how far it is a safe and sufficient *guide* in pointing out that conduct, which, according to my idea of virtue, is virtuous conduct.

Dr. *Paley*, Book II. Chap. 6. says, "Whatever is expedient, is right. It is the utility of any moral rule alone, which constitutes the obligation of it." Now, with respect to the latter of these two sentences, I might observe, that Dr. *Paley*, consistently with what he had previously said respecting the *ground of obligation,*

obligation, could not say, that the general utility of any moral rule constitutes the *obligation* of it. He had before said (how justly I do not now consider) that obligation arises from a regard to our *own* happiness. If it be alledged, that he probably intended to say here, that " it is the utility of any moral rule alone, which constitutes the *rectitude* of it;" and that it is an error in *writing*, rather than in *thinking*, it might still be urged, that since, admitting Dr. *Paley*'s principles, general utility denotes rectitude, only as it is indicative of the will of God, it is the *mark*, not the *constituent* of rectitude. Accordingly, understanding him to mean no more, than that utility, considered as expressing the will of God, is the rule of virtue, of which moralists have so long been in quest, let us examine the justness of that opinion. I do not
hesitate

hesitate to allow, that a regard to utility, especially when explained, as it is explained by Dr. *Paley*, with reference to *general consequences*, is a very *extensive* rule of right conduct; that it is *one* good rule among others*: but I contend against its being considered as of *universal* application; not only lest it should thence be rested in as the *ground* of virtue, to the prejudice of our moral *principle*; but also from the danger, in many instances, of its directing us to wrong *conduct*. From the *benevolence* of God, which

may

---

* How far men, even when acting virtuously, have really acted, or can be expected to act, with any regard to general consequences, may still be questioned. When the *Athenians* rejected the proposal of *Themistocles* to set fire to the *Spartan* fleet, because, in the judgment of *Aristides*, though a *useful*, it was not an *honest* enterprize, they did not, I suppose, reject it on the principle, that, though useful in that particular instance, it would not be so to them, or to the world at large, " upon the *whole*, and at the *long run*." See the case in *Cicero's* Off. B. III. C. 11.

may be so satisfactorily made out from the creation and government of the world, and which has been so satisfactorily made out by Dr. *Paley**, we may indeed justly

---

* In saying this, I do not intend to admit, that a chapter on *divine benevolence*, however excellent in itself, properly forms any part of a system of Morality. In *Morality*, the being and attributes of God are to be taken as proved. The proof of them, whether *(a priori)* by metaphysical arguments, or *(a posteriori)* by physical ones, i.e. by deduction from the works of creation and providence, belongs to *Natural Religion*.

For the full discussion of this important part of Natural Religion (the benevolence of God) see the invaluable tract of the late Dr. *Balguy*, entitled, " Divine benevolence asserted, and vindicated from the objections of ancient and modern sceptics." How much is it to be lamented, that the work, of which that tract, printed in 1781, is said by the author to be a *specimen*, has not yet (I write in 1798) been published! In a pecuniary view, indeed, such publications, from the improbability of their becoming *popular*, may not answer to the publishers; but it is pity, that those, who are capable of understanding and relishing them, should therefore be hindered from their use. In the present case, however, I have no doubt, that the Syndics of the *Cambridge* press, ever ready to promote the interests of sound learning and religion, would afford their assistance

justly conclude, that God wills the happiness of his creatures, and that, in the promotion of this end, he wills the co-operation of all intelligent beings, according to their several abilities of promoting it. But whether, in order to the promotion of this end, the end itself ought to be the sole *rule* of our conduct, situated as we are, is an entirely different question: It is evident, that, in many instances, we are very incompetent judges of what *will* promote general happiness. Several writers of eminence, among whom I wish

to

---

in bringing before the public *such* a work of *such* a son of their common *alma mater*, and would even esteem it an honour to do so.

To those, who have been informed of what passed at a particular *meeting* of the Syndics, respecting the present publication, it may seem, that the above passage is intended to be understood in an *ironical* and *sarcastic* sense. I think it necessary to declare, therefore, that it stands exactly as it did before the transaction referred to took place.

to particularize Bishop *Butler* and Mr. *Gisborne*, have given very forcible reasons why *utility*, as judged of by such short-sighted beings as we are, ought not to be considered as the criterion of virtuous conduct. As this is a point of considerable importance, it may be worth while to give their reasons in their own words.

Bishop *Butler*, in his *Dissertation on Virtue*, says, "Some authors of distinguished merit have, I think, expressed themselves in a manner, which may occasion some danger to careless readers of imagining, that the whole of virtue consists in singly aiming, according to the best of their judgment, at promoting the happiness of mankind in the present state; and the whole of vice in doing what they foresee, or might foresee, is likely to produce

duce an overbalance of unhappiness in it; than which mistakes, none can be conceived more terrible. For it is certain, that some of the most shocking instances of injustice, adultery, murder, perjury, and even of persecution, may, in many supposeable cases, not have the appearance of being likely to produce an overbalance of misery in the present state: sometimes, perhaps, may have the contrary appearance. This reflection might easily be carried on; but I forbear.--- The happiness of the world is the concern of him, who is the lord and proprietor of it. Nor do we know what we are about, when we endeavour to promote the good of mankind in any ways but those, which he has directed.---Though it is our business and our duty to endeavour, within the bounds of veracity and justice, to contribute to the ease, convenience, and

even

even chearfulness and diversion of our fellow-creatures; yet, from our short views, it is greatly uncertain whether this endeavour will, in particular instances, produce an overbalance of happiness upon the whole; since so many and distant things must come into the account."

Mr. *Gisborne*, in his *Principles of Moral Philosophy investigated*, has made many judicious remarks to nearly the same purpose, and in a manner still more full. The whole of Part I. is, indeed, so directly in point, that I should not well know how to limit a transcript from it. After giving two or three of the most striking passages, therefore, I must refer the reader to the work itself. " From the very principle of divine benevolence," he observes, " on which Mr. *Paley*'s doctrine of of general expediency is founded, we muſt be convinced, that our Maker would never ſubject his creatures to the guidance of a rule, which it is impoſſible for them to comprehend, and conſequently to obey. A moment's reflection muſt teach us, that ſuch is the rule propoſed by Mr. *Paley*. General expediency is an inſtrument not to be wielded by a mortal hand. The nature of general conſequences is too comprehenſive to be embraced by human underſtanding, too dark to be penetrated by human diſcernment." Afterwards alſo, having referred to an interpretation of Dr. *Paley*'s ſyſtem, which amounts to a confeſſion, that, in practice, we are not to look to general expediency in that comprehenſive ſenſe, which is " beyond the reach of our faculties; but that our actions are to be regulated by what appears to us to be expedient, as far as we can

can *discern* their probable consequences;" he adds, " Our experience of God's dispensations by no means permits us to affirm, that he always thinks fit to act in such a manner, as is productive of particular expediency; much less to conclude, that he wills us always to act in such a manner, as *we* suppose would be productive of it." I quote from the first edition of this work, not being able to procure any other: but I understand, that, in a subsequent edition or editions, it has been considerably enlarged and improved*.

That

---

* See also an elegant and impressive tract, lately published, entitled, " An Examination of the leading principle of the new system of morals, as that principle is stated and applied in Mr. *Godwin*'s Enquiry concerning Political Justice;" in which is clearly shown, by a reference to Mr. *Godwin*'s publication, as a complete exemplification of the new system of morals, what practical effects may reasonably

That God is *benevolent*, there is no doubt; but, that benevolence forms the *whole* and *exclusive* moral character of God, who will presume to say? And, even supposing this to be the case, we do not know all the ways, by which benevolence, in order to produce its greatest effect, is to be exerted. We are certain, however, that God does not always exert it by promoting the present pleasure or happiness of each individual, but often by a long series of painful trials. For these trials,

reasonably be expected from the universal adoption of the principle of utility as the *ground* of moral obligation, or even as the *rule* of moral conduct. It would be a compliment to my own undertaking to say, that I consider a work, in which so much acumen and so great a knowledge of the subject are displayed, as a proper preliminary evidence of the need of such an one, as *(qualicunque Minervâ)* I have here attempted. The *remedy*, indeed, which the author prescribes for the evil, of which he seems so justly sensible, and which he so forcibly describes, is different from that, which I have provided. Which of the two is most likely to be effectual, others must determine.

trials, admitting the moral government of God, muſt be conſidered as proceeding from him, whether they are brought on by the inſtrumentality of men, or not; and how long, in each particular caſe, they ought to be continued, or with what degree of ſeverity inflicted, it is not in the power of man to determine. Beſides, therefore, the difficulty of diſcovering, in many caſes, what actions are conducive to the general good, which Dr. *Paley* himſelf, in ſaying (Book VI. Chap. 12.) that " it is impoſſible to aſcertain every duty by an immediate reference to public utility," ſeems to allow, there are additional objections againſt admitting a regard to it as an *univerſal* criterion of virtue; ſuch objections, indeed, as are ſufficient to awaken the caution of every one, who is really *deſirous* of promoting general good. Enough has been ſaid to ſhow,

show, that it is at least an imperfect and inadequate rule of virtue; that, throwing a snare in the way of the unguarded, it exposes the well-disposed to the danger of doing evil, that good may come; and that, to the ill-disposed, it affords a plausible pretext for doing absolute wrong.

With respect to the *moral sense*, I admit its reality; but, having already excluded it from being the *ground* of moral obligation, I now deny its sufficiency (either as it is the gift of nature, or as it actually exists in the generality of men) to be the *rule* of it. I do not consider it as a matter of much consequence to the interests of morality to enquire, whether the moral sense be implanted by nature, or whether it be the sole effect of culture. It is a question, which belongs

to

to *metaphysics*, rather than to *morality*. I am of opinion, however, that it *is* implanted by nature. I conceive, that the human mind, the work of God, and made in the *image* of God, is so constituted as to approve those actions, when presented to it, which are agreeable to the *will* of God, and to disapprove those, which are not; that it is formed, in short, to the approbation of right, and the disapprobation of wrong. Let it not be understood, that this formation implies *innate ideas*. All that is meant by it is, that, when the mind comes to be exercised about such or such ideas, it is so formed as to make such or such determinations respecting them. The sentiment of compassion, for instance, (considered as an *effect* of the moral sense), though not itself innate, may yet arise *naturally*, that is, as the *dictate of nature*, as soon as the idea of undeserved suffering is presented to the mind. Such a formation of the mind no more implies any innate ideas of moral actions, than the formation of the mind to an agreement with *intellectual* truths, when they are presented to it, implies innate ideas of the objects, to which those truths relate. When a person is brought to a perception of the ideas belonging to any proposition in Euclid, and to attend to their relation, his conviction of their relation follows as a natural and necessary result; he does not, he cannot, think differently about it from other persons. As soon as the mind is shown (*properly* shown) the relation between two right angles and the three angles of a triangle, it necessarily, from its own nature and constitution, assents to the equality between them. Here, the faculty of judging

may

may be considered as innate, as part of the constitution of the mind; though, certainly, none of the *ideas* are innate. In like manner, as soon as the mind is presented with the idea of an action, which is truly virtuous (by whatever means ascertained to be so) it may approve it, without having the idea of that action, or indeed *any* idea, previously impressed*. Thus, the belief of an innate moral sense, as asserted by Mr. *Hutcheson*, Bishop *Butler*, and others, is not inconsistent, as some have seemed to understand it, with the opinion so ably maintained by Mr. *Locke*,

---

* We may observe, by the way, that, in proportion as we distinguish right and wrong by means of the moral sense, the *knowledge* of our duty is forced upon us, however free we may still be as to the *practice* of it. In this, indeed, is supposed, what is not likely often to happen, that the action is presented to the mind in a *simple* state, disentangled from that perplexity of circumstances, in which human actions are generally involved.

*Locke**, and ever since so generally received, that we have no *innate ideas*. "We are not to imagine," says Mr. *Hutcheson*, " that this *moral sense*, more than the other senses, supposes any innate ideas, or knowledge, or practical proposition. We mean by it only a determination of our minds to receive amiable or disagreeable ideas of actions, when they shall occur to our observation, antecedently to any opinions of advantage or

loss

---

* Mr. *Locke* was not the first, who held this opinion. His Essay was first published in 1688 or 1689. Bishop *Pearson*, in his excellent Exposition of the Creed, which was first published in 1659, says, " I rather conceive the soul of man to have no connatural knowledge at all, no particular notion of any thing in it from the beginning; but, since we can have no assurance of its pre-existence, we may more rationally judge it to receive the first apprehensions of things by *sense*, and by them to make all rational collections. If then the soul of man be, at the first, like a fair smooth table, without any actual characters of knowledge imprinted on it; if all the knowledge we have comes successively by sensation, instruction, and rational collection, &c." Article, I believe in *God*.

loss to redound to ourselves from them; even as we are pleased with a *regular form*, or an *harmonious composition*, without having any knowledge of mathematics, or seeing any advantage in that form or composition, different from the immediate pleasure." The mind may originally have a taste or turn for virtue, by which, without having any ideas, it may be prepared to approve of certain actions, and to disapprove of others, just as (to use another analogy) our bodily organs are prepared to relish particular objects in such or such a way, without our having any previous ideas of the objects themselves. Accordingly, Mr. *Locke* himself, the great assertor of the doctrine of *no innate ideas*, does not deny, that " there are natural *tendencies* imprinted on the minds of men; and that, from the very first instances of sense and perception,

perception, there are some things that are grateful, and others unwelcome to them; some things that they incline to, and others that they fly." I the rather dwell on this, because Dr. *Paley* has observed, that, to maintain the existence of a *moral sense*, and the existence of *innate maxims*, is the same thing; an assertion, which, in my opinion, is calculated to excite a prejudice of a very dangerous nature. Whether, in fact, the mind be so formed or not, can be determined with certainty only by *experience*; and it is a case, in which experience cannot be consulted. The supposition referred to by Dr. *Paley* of a human being, who, without any instruction or moral discipline, should be arrived at the use of reason, and be called upon to decide on a moral case, as a test whether the moral sense be the gift of nature, or not, involves in it something

like

like a contradiction; it not being possible to bring the case before him without giving him a considerable degree of previous instruction. I have, however, already observed, that it is not material to the present inquiry, whether the moral sense be considered as innate or acquired. Whatever be its *origin*, I admit (nay, insist on) its *reality*. Dr. *Balguy (Divine Benevolence asserted*, p. 140.) says, "It is difficult to conceive how it can have happened, that the *reality* of these sentiments (speaking of sentiments arising from the *moral sense*, or *moral faculty*) should ever have been disputed. They are not indeed *innate*; for *no* sentiments are innate. But they are *common*, I suppose, to our whole species." Perhaps, however, the dispute has not been so much about the *reality* of the sentiments, as about their *origin*; and not so much

about

about the origin of the *sentiments*, as of the faculty of receiving them, i. e. the *moral sense*. Probably also this is the meaning, in which the dispute is *intended* to be referred to by Dr. *Paley*; though, by what he has inadvertently said, he may seem to disparage the moral sense as existing in men at any period of their life.

Be the question of an *innate* moral sense, then, decided as it may, no doubt need be entertained, that every mind, which has received any degree of moral culture, is possessed of a moral sense. It is the object of such culture to form it where it either was not originally, or is obliterated (if that be possible) by vicious conduct, and to improve it where it is. Dr. *Balguy* adds, very justly, I think, that " probably there never was a single man, who

who was void of all perception of right and wrong*." But, afferting the *reality* of the moral fenfe, I deny its fufficiency to the purpofes of morality. I deny it altogether as the *foundation* of virtue, and I deny it an *exclufive* claim to be the *rule*. Actions, which are dictated by that fenfe, and which proceed from it as a principle, are not, properly fpeaking, *virtuous* actions, nor the objects of pofitive reward. They are, indeed, the evidence of a virtuous *difpofition* or habit of mind, which it is the intention of a courfe of virtuous actions to produce; but, in proportion as it is produced, the idea of obligation vanifhes, and duty and

immediate

---

* " When the Gentiles, which have not the law, do by nature the things contained in the law, thefe, having not the law, are a law unto themfelves : Which fhow the work of the law written in their hearts, their confcience alfo bearing witnefs, and their thoughts, the mean while, accufing, or elfe excufing one another." *Rom.* 2. xiv, xv.

immediate happiness unite. This, as I conceive, is the state and happiness of *Angels*; which, indeed, seems to coincide with the general notion respecting them; for it is not, I think, ordinarily understood, that Angels, though they are supposed constantly to obey the will of God, perform actions, which can properly be called *virtuous* actions.* In short, virtue and vice have a necessary relation to a state of *discipline*; to that state, in which the agents, by a series of particular actions, are gradually formed to a *character* either of virtue or of vice, of goodness or badness;

after

---

* That is, in the same sense, in which the actions of *human* beings in a state of *discipline* are called virtuous. I have thought it right, however, so to frame the definition of virtue, as to make it comprehend the right conduct of created and dependent beings in every stage of their existence; leaving out, as matter of separate consideration, all regard to the *motive*, by which each, according to the degree of his moral improvement, may be urged to the observance of that conduct.

after which, their actions become the *natural*, not to say *necessary*, effect of their respective characters. This idea, if I mistake not, opens to us the whole business of morality, and the design of the different situations, in which we are here placed, calculated, as they evidently are, to call forth the different virtues into use, and to improve them into lasting habits.

If, then, it be the *end* of virtue to bring the moral sense to perfection, it will scarcely be thought, that the moral sense itself, in its progress towards perfection, was intended to be the sole *means*, by which virtue is to be ascertained; though, so far as it is the gift of nature, and in proportion to its improvement, it may be *one* useful means of ascertaining virtue, and promoting its practice. Besides, it is pretty evident, from the different

sentiments

sentiments entertained of the same actions by different persons, according to the degree of cultivation, to which the moral sense has been brought in them; that this sense, as it exists in the generality of men, is by no means a *certain* criterion of virtue, nor one, to which, in all cases, they can safely trust. The final cause why it is not of itself a sufficient guide has been already suggested; and may, perhaps, appear still more clearly afterwards. Here, I shall only add, that the *immediate* cause may be, that it is not consistent with the nature of the moral sense to manifest the same *degree* of approbation and disapprobation at different virtues or vices; consequently, its operation is not always equally sensible. In some cases, its dictates force themselves on the most inattentive: in others, they are perceptible by those only,

only, who are in the habit of listening to its voice.

The result is, that, in order to act virtuously, we must always have in view obedience to the will of God; but that, in order to discover what his will is, with respect to any particular action, we are not confined to *one* mark or criterion of it, but are at liberty to make use of any of the methods, by which, as we conceive, it may be discovered with the greatest ease and certainty. Different men, according to their respective habits, and according to the nature of the case, may safely have recourse to the rule of general utility, conformity to truth or the eternal differences of things, the moral sense, or any other rule of similar tendency, as each may be of more convenient application, so long as it is, and is *considered* to be,

expressive

expressive of the will of God. Even the same person, at different times, and on different occasions, may be permitted to say, 'This action is conformable to the natural differences of things; this is agreeable to truth; this has a tendency to general good; this is the result of my sense of right and wrong; and so on;' and may thence justly conclude, with respect to each of them, that it is agreeable to the will of God, and therefore a virtuous action. If he proceed to *act* under that persuasion, he acts virtuously; but, if I mistake not, where there is no reference, immediate or mediate, to the will of God, there, whatever may be the *rule* of action, and whatever may be the *action*, there is no *virtue**.

I conclude

---

* From the admission of a *variety* of rules of virtue, rather than an exclusive *one*, there results at least this advantage,

I conclude this Chapter with observing, that if, in the course of it, I have not discovered a criterion or rule of virtue, which is of universal application, I have perhaps shown, what may prevent disappointment in the future search for it, that such a criterion is not to be discovered. I was led to the subject of this Chapter, as expressed in the title of it, rather (in conformity with the character of a *remarker*) by what had been attempted by others, than by what I had any intention of attempting myself; rather with the view of showing what could *not* be done, than with the expectation of doing it*.

advantage, that one good work on the subject of morality need not be considered as superseding another. *Clarke*, *Wollaston*, *Hutcheson*, *Paley*, &c. &c. are *all* useful in their several ways, *all* to be read, *all* to be respected.

* I would not altogether discourage *speculation*; but I cannot help thinking, that it would be useful to put speculation under a greater check than it is under at present. I acknowledge, with sentiments of high respect, that many

writers

writers of the prefent day, purfuing the legitimate mode of philofophical inveftigation, have made great advances in real knowledge; yet I can eafily conceive, that an obferver, who fhould form his judgment from fome recent publications of celebrity, and fome prevalent opinions in confequence, might conclude, that our courfe of late has been *retrograde*. At the clofe of this century, we have not, generally fpeaking, attained to much practical proficiency in the important leffon, which Mr. *Locke* taught us at the clofe of the laft, and for the elucidation of which he wrote his immortal *Effay*; namely, " to prevail with the bufy mind of man to be more cautious in meddling with things exceeding its comprehenfion; to ftop, when it is at the utmoft extent of its tether; and to fit down in a quiet ignorance of thofe things, which, upon examination, are found to be beyond the reach of our capacities." The greateft minds can hope to make no progrefs beyond certain *limits*, nor within thofe limits but by proper *methods*. How different is even *Newton*, when tracing the motions of the planets and of the fea, a fubject of obfervation and calculation, to the principle of Gravitation as their caufe, and when attempting to trace the caufe of Gravitation itfelf to an ætherial medium, on which no *experiments* could be made! In the one cafe, he is an accurate and profound reafoner, developing the moft aftonifhing truths; in the other, a mere conjecturer, and on a level with his fellow-mortals. See Qu. 21, at the end of his *Optics*, compared with the end of his *Principia*. *Newton*, however, ever preferving the character of a true philofopher, has the modefty to propofe his conjectures *as* conjectures, not as matters of fcience. See the fecond Advertifement to his *Optics*.

CHAP.

CHAP. III.

ON THE OBLIGATION TO OBTAIN THE *KNOWLEDGE* OF VIRTUE.

THE obligation to obtain the *knowledge* of virtue, or (what, according to my scheme, is the same thing) of endeavouring to *discover* the will of God, is exactly of the same kind with that, which lies upon us to obey it when discovered. It arises entirely, as that does, from the powers, with which we are furnished by God, and the relation, in which we stand to him, as our maker and preserver. We may add, indeed, that the one is virtually contained in the other. For since, without knowing the will of God, it is impossible

to

to obey it, at least with the intention of doing so, the obligation to obey it implies the obligation to employ our abilities in the search of it. Reason is the appointed guide, by which we are to find out what the will of God is. Some of the methods, in which reason is to be employed for this purpose, have been considered in the preceding Chapter; where it was also observed, that, since no one method is of equally convenient application to every case, nor equally suited to different persons, we are at liberty to make use of that, which is best adapted to lead us, with ease and certainty, to the object in view. There seems no other reason for preferring one method before another. The virtue of an action is the same, supposing it to proceed from the principle of obeying the will of God, whatever be the method, by which it is ascertained to be so.

Let

Let it be observed, that, when I speak of *ascertaining* the will of God respecting human actions, I do not mean the attaining to a *demonstrative* knowledge of it; but only to that assurance of it, which is grounded on *probability*, and which, indeed, as I conceive, is better suited to answer the purposes of morality, than demonstration itself. I am of opinion, not only that there is no *one* certain method of discovering the will of God; but that it cannot, strictly speaking, be *certainly* discovered at all. In other words, I do not think, that morality is matter of *demonstration*. It is our duty to obey the will of God, according to the knowledge we have of it; and it is our duty, by all the powers and means afforded us, to seek for the knowledge of it: but there is, I think, no ground to suppose, that, by any of the powers and

means

means afforded us, we can attain to a *demonstrative* knowledge of it. Had there been any thing of the nature of demonstration belonging to morality, it is scarcely to be conceived, that there would have been that diversity of opinions, respecting many parts of it, which we actually find. It is well known, however, that Mr. *Locke*, whom, on such a subject, it is hazardous to oppose, thinks, that morality is capable of demonstration. He alledges, that " the ideas, about which Ethics are conversant, being all real essences, and such as have a discoverable connection and agreement with each other; so far as we discover their habitudes and relations, so far we shall be possessed of certain, real, and general truths." Granting the premises to be true, we should certainly be obliged to admit the conclusion. But the granting of them, I think, supposes, that

that morality arises from the relation between our ideas of human actions arbitrarily formed, without reference to what may be the will of God respecting them. Our ideas of human actions, so far as they are made by the mind, are indeed real essences, and we may be able, with certainty, to discover the relation between them. It is not, however, about the relation of these ideas among themselves, that morality is employed; but about the relation between them and our ideas of God's will respecting them; and our ideas of God's will respecting them, though real essences also, may yet, as applied to what his will respecting them really is, be either true or false. So that, though an abstract system of morality, depending on the relation of ideas arbitrarily formed in the mind, be capable of demonstration; yet the case is very different

ferent with respect to a system of morality, which, like that binding on human beings, has reference to something extraneous to the mind. Though, in this case, our ideas of relation be ever so just, our conclusions respecting them, as applicable to human conduct, will be true or false, according as our notions of God's will are true or false. Mr. *Locke* had before said, " The idea of a supreme Being, infinite in power, goodness, and wisdom, whose *workmanship* we are, and on whom we *depend*; and the idea of ourselves, as understanding rational Beings, being such as are clear in us, would, I suppose, if duly considered and pursued, afford such foundations of our duty and rules of action, as might place *morality among the sciences capable of demonstration:* wherein I doubt not, but from self-evident propositions, by necessary consequences,

quences, as incontestable as those in Mathematics, the measures of right and wrong might be made out to any one, that will apply himself with the same indifferency and attention to the one, as he does to the other of these sciences." This passage, if I mistake not, so far from proving what it was intended to prove, furnishes the *reason* why we are not to number morality among the sciences capable of demonstration; for it admits the necessity, to this purpose, of our having that certainty respecting our ideas of God and of his will, which we have not the power of obtaining. The only method, by which we can arrive at those ideas, is by *revelation*, or by *deduction from the works of creation and providence**; and, in

---

* Under this head are included all those indications of the divine will, respecting human actions, which may be

collected

in either case, whether they are true or false, can never be more than matter of probability. Mr. *Locke* does, indeed, give instances in two propositions, which, he thinks, are as certain as any demonstrations in Euclid. One is, "Where there is no property, there is no injustice." The other, "No government allows absolute liberty." But, though it should be granted, that both these propositions are demonstrably true, it might still be contended, that neither of them implies any reference to the will of God, an essential part of the idea of virtue; and, consequently, that neither of them, properly speaking, is a rule of virtue, or a

part

---

collected from the consideration of the temporal rewards, which generally, and according to the natural tendency of things, follow some of them, and the punishments, which as generally and naturally follow others. This subject is discussed, with admirable force and effect, in the immortal *Analogy* of Bishop *Butler*. See, particularly, his Chapter on the "Moral Government of God."

part of morality. In truth, they are propositions, which teach no other knowledge than that of the *signification of terms*, and are what Mr. *Locke* calls *trifling* propositions*. But, whether Mr. *Locke*, in his attempt to fhow, that morality is capable of demonstration, has succeeded or not, he has at least pointed out, in this paffage, the true method of ftudying morality; that is, obtaining juft notions of the will of God, and applying them to human conduct. This, as I conceive, is the only method, by which morality can be carried to that degree of perfection, of which it is capable. I may further obferve, by the way, that, in deducing moral duties from the relation between the divine will and human actions, and making true notions of that will neceffary to a true morality, he here

again

---

* See his *Effay*, Book IV. Chap. 8.

again agrees with me, in resting on it the *foundation* of morality.

" Probable evidence," says Bishop *Butler*, " is essentially distinguished from demonstration by this, that it admits of *degrees*; and of all variety of them, from the highest moral certainty, to the very lowest presumption." When the truth of a mathematical proposition is once made out, by a just and legitimate demonstration, we are as much convinced of its truth, as we should be after seeing it demonstrated a thousand times, and in a thousand different ways; whereas our conviction of a truth built on probability, being susceptible of various degrees, rises, in proportion to the number and strength of the arguments, from the slightest presumption to the confines of absolute certainty. From this account of the

distinction

distinction between probable and demonstrative evidence, we may, I think, discover the *final* cause why no moral rule holds universally, and why morality itself is not matter of strict demonstration. For, from this constitution of things, there results this evident advantage, that, in the investigation of moral truth, there is indispensable need of a *sincere and honest mind*, patient to attend to every argument, which may be offered, and ready to give each its proper weight; an advantage peculiarly adapted to beings placed, as we are, in a state of probation and discipline. The exercise of balancing opposing evidence must greatly improve our intellectual powers; and the temptations, which immediate interest, or the desire of gratifying our passions, sometimes affords, of leaning to the less evidence rather than to the greater, must, if happily

pily overcome, strengthen and establish our virtue. It seems to me, therefore, that it was never the intention of the author of our nature, that *moral* truths should admit of the same kind of proof as *mathematical* ones; but that, depending on *accumulative* evidence, they should rise higher and higher in credibility, rewarding our industry and integrity by continual approaches to that certainty, which yet we shall never attain. We are not, however, to conclude from this, that the conviction, which is thus obtained, of moral truth, is necessarily less satisfactory to the mind, than if it were obtained by mathematical demonstration. The evidence, by which it is furnished, is a tower, whose height increases by every moment's observation and reflection; and, though the foundation of it be humbly laid in the dust, the top soon ascends beyond the

reach

reach of the eye, and is lost amidst the clouds*.

Be this, however, as it may: whatever may be the effect, with which reason is exerted, it is, as I have already said, the natural and appointed teacher, by which we are to be instructed in what the will of God is. How far reason alone was a *sufficient* guide for the purpose, it was the province of experience to determine. Accordingly, the experience of the heathen

---

* See a *Note* to the tenth of my "Discourses to Academic Youth." To those, who are desirous of confirmation or illustration of what is here said, with respect to the force of evidence built on probability, I earnestly recommend the perusal of Bishop *Taylor*'s "Moral Demonstration of the Truth of the Christian Religion, with an Introduction on the Nature and Force of probable Arguments," originally published as part of his *Ductor Dubitantium* (Book I. Chap. 4. Rule ii.) and since republished, in a separate form, by Bishop *Hurd*. The second Edition of the republication was printed for *T. Cadell*, in 1776. I am indebted, for the thought of this recommendation, to the suggestion of a judicious friend.

heathen world abundantly evinced the advantage, not to say necessity, of such additional information respecting the divine will, as we understand by a *revelation* of it from heaven. I have already noticed the ignorance, in which, from whatever cause, the generality of the heathens were, respecting the will of God; as likewise the confession, which was made by one of the wisest among them*, of the necessity of further information on this subject, than mere reason could furnish. Sir *Isaac Newton* very justly observes, (*Optics*, near the end) that, " so far as we can know by natural philosophy what is the first cause, what power he has over us, and what benefits we receive from him, so far our duty towards him, as well as that towards one another, will appear to us by the light of nature;" and it may thence

---

* *Plato* under the character of *Socrates*.

thence, perhaps, be concluded, that, in confequence of the great difcoveries, which have been made in natural philofophy in modern days, the improvements in moral philofophy, which are attributed to revelation, might have been made by the light of nature. This conclufion, however, is by no means juft. No doubt, the perfection of natural philofophy in all its parts, as referred to by Sir *Ifaac Newton*, will tend to enlarge the bounds of moral philofophy alfo*; yet it may juftly be contended, that there are many parts of morality, as taught by revelation, which are entirely independent of an accurate knowledge of nature. The original nature, depravation, mode of reftoration, and final deftination of the human

---

* That is, agreeably to the diftinction made in page 7, improvements in *natural philofophy* would produce improvements in *natural religion*, and thefe again improvements in *morality*.

human race, are subjects, on which the greatest discoveries in natural knowledge could throw but little light. It may further be observed, and the observation merits particular attention, that the heathens failed in drawing that deduction relating to morality, to which, as we should now judge, the most obvious parts of natural knowledge, and such as certainly obtained among them, were sufficient to lead them; namely, the *goodness of God.* On the supposition of an all-powerful and perfectly benevolent Deity, the mixture of good and evil in the present life of man was a paradox, which, in all probability, reason alone would never have been able to explain. It is an error to imagine, that morality, as we find it in modern systems, though apparently made out on the grounds of reasoning, is the sole effect of

reason,

reason, or is what reason, if left to itself, would ever have been able to discover. Moral duties, when proposed to us, may become deducible from the principles of reason; though they could not, perhaps, by reason have been originally traced out; just as we cannot but admit the truth of a mathematical demonstration, when proposed and explained to us, which yet, without the help of a better invention than our own, we should never have been able to discover. The *morality* of the Gospel, as matter of science, has extended beyond its *authority*; and many, who shut their eyes to its immediate rays, have been directed by its reflected light. " Many arguments, many truths, both moral and religious, which appear to us the products of our understandings, and the fruits of ratiocination, are, in reality, nothing more than emanations from

Scripture,

Scripture, rays of the Gospel imperceptibly transmitted, and, as it were, conveyed to our minds in a side light. Many of our deductions and discoveries, which we are apt to look upon as the oracles of our reason, would be found, if they were fairly traced, entirely owing to certain hints borrowed from revelation*." We must not, then, from the delineation of moral duties, as we have them drawn by *Christian* pencils, take our idea of what unassisted reason could discover concerning them. We are also to take into account, that some light, respecting the truths of morality, might shine from the *Jewish* tabernacle, confined as it was to a particular people and country, on the world at large; that many of the maxims, which

---

* See the second Letter to a Deist, in " Tracts moral and theological, by *John Balguy*, M. A. Vicar of North-Allerton, *Yorkshire*."

which gave celebrity to heathen philosophers, probably had their origin in the inspired regulations of *Moses*.

Dr. *Paley* represents Mr. *Hume* as "complaining of the modern scheme of uniting Ethics with the Christian Theology." Now, there is a sense, in which this may be *justly* complained of; that is, when, in a scientific treatise on the subject, moral duties, without being made to appear such by reasoning from the principles of the science, are made to rest on the mere *authority* of revelation; when, in short, the Scriptures are considered as the *foundation* of moral obligation. This, I admit, is not only an infringement of the laws of good writing, but a perversion of the natural order of things; for, in truth, the Scriptures themselves become to us an obligatory rule

rule of life, only as they are made out on evidence, of which reason is the judge, to be declaratory of the will of God. The Scriptures reveal to us *facts*, existing relations between God and us, arising from his nature and our nature, which we either should not have known, or should not have attended to, had they not been revealed to us; but, when once these are known, the duties, which result from them, may be made out on grounds of reason, and therefore ought to be so made out by those, who profess to explain morality scientifically*. But, when Mr. *Hume*

---

* Thus, if it were said, 'This action is commanded in Scripture, and therefore it is your duty to do it', I should not think this a proper way of teaching morality *scientifically*. But, if it were said, 'This duty is the result of a relation, which is made known to us in Scripture', and if the result were properly made out by reasoning, my objection would cease. To some, this may seem a distinction *too nice*; but it certainly is not so in a *scientific* view.

Perhaps

Hume complains of use being made, in the science of morality, of those relations between

Perhaps it will not seem so in a more *popular* view, when it is considered, that the reason, why many precepts of Scripture are not now esteemed as obligatory on us, is founded on this distinction. Morality, considered as a science, may proceed on truths, of which the proof belongs to *revealed religion*, just as it does on truths, of which the proof belongs to *natural religion*. The proof of the being and attributes of God, such as they are discoverable to be by reason, belongs to natural religion; but the duties thence arising are, properly speaking, *moral* duties. So the duties, which arise from the truth, that men obtain salvation only through the merits of Christ, are *moral* duties, though the proof of that truth belongs to revealed religion. See Bishop *Butler's* Analogy, Part II. Chap. 1. It is to be remembered, however, that all the unabrogated precepts of Scripture are *obligatory* on those, who acknowledge it as a revelation from heaven, even though (as some contend is the case of the precept respecting the observance of a Sabbath*) they cannot be made out to be so on the grounds of reason; and it will easily be allowed, that the *ten Commandments*, when considered as an *authoritative* declaration of God's will, are far more effectual to the teaching of morality than the finest systems of the heathen world.

* That is, they contend, that, admitting the fact of God's having created the world in six days, and rested from creation on the seventh, it does not follow, on the principles of *reason*, that we are bound to observe an hebdomadal rest.

between God and us, which revelation makes known to us, by deducing from them the duties, which naturally refult from them, he complains unjuftly. With equal reafon might he complain of ufe being made, in the fcience of *Natural Philofophy*, of the new facts, which experiments are perpetually difclofing, by making deductions from them refpecting the powers of nature. It is, as I conceive, with ftill lefs reafon, that he objects to the production of thofe *motives* to virtuous practice, which, whether otherwife difcoverable or not, were actually difcovered only by revelation.

Revelation may be confidered in two important (it need not be decided whether *equally* important) points of view; as *teaching* us our duty, and as furnifhing us with *motives* to perform it. The
latter

latter we shall have occasion to consider in the Chapter on the *motive to virtue*. With respect to the former, we may here more particularly observe, that, since men have very different opinions of the same action, as to its being virtuous or the contrary, and especially as to the *degree* of its being so, according to their acquaintance with the will of God, and since their acquaintance with his will must depend on their notions of his nature, the nature of man, and the consequent relation between them, to all of which we must suppose the divine will to have respect, the revelation, which has credible pretensions to the ability of giving us information on those points, cannot properly, even in a system of *rational* Ethics, be passed over without notice*. It may be added, that, though

* The vast importance of just notions of the divine nature may be collected from the circumstance, that, to
declare

morality is *principally* taught in the Scriptures, by making known to us these facts in a clearer light than men either *did* or *could* know them without a revelation; yet, particularly in what relates to the due regulation of the *thoughts*, it is also taught there, in a manner very highly to be valued, by *positive precepts.* Dr. *Paley* says, that " the Scriptures are employed, not so much to teach new *rules* of morality, as to enforce the practice

---

declare the nature and attributes of the true and only God, in opposition to the notions, which the heathens entertained of their Gods, was the primary object of the Patriarchal and Mosaic dispensations. The reader, besides, will not fail to recollect, as a testimony from experience to the same purpose, the actual effect, which heathen *theology* had on heathen *manners.* " No doubt," says Sir *Isaac Newton,* " if the worship of false Gods had not blinded the heathens, their moral philosophy would have gone further than to the four cardinal virtues; and, instead of teaching the transmigration of souls, and to worship the sun and moon, and dead heroes, they would have taught us to worship our true author and benefactor." *Optics,* end of the Queries.

tice of it by new *sanctions*, and by a *greater certainty*; which last seems to be the proper business of a revelation from God, and what was most wanted." Without controverting the truth of this; without attempting to decide in what view revelation is of *most* importance; I may safely venture to affirm, that Dr. *Paley* himself, in his Chapter on the *morality of the Gospel**, by his own observations, and by the judicious use which he has made of Mr. *Soame Jenyns*' "Internal evidence of Christianity," has given most satisfactory proof, that the Scriptures teach morality with a sublimity and impression, to which no human method of teaching it can make pretensions. Whoever reads that Chapter with the attention, which is due to it,

cannot

---

* See his excellent " View of the Evidences of Christianity."

cannot fail, I think, to be convinced of the *excellence* of the Gospel, whatever he may think of its *truth**.

On the whole, then, it is our duty to search for the will of God wherever there is any probability of our being able to discover it, and diligently to employ, for that purpose, *all* the powers and means, which we possess or can procure. In order to become what *Cicero* calls "boni ratiocinatores officiorum," we must pursue the method, which he prescribes, and which, so far as he had opportunity, he himself seems to have pursued; "consuetudo exercitatioque capienda est†."

For

---

* The reader may also consult, with no less profit than pleasure, that part of the celebrated profession of faith of the Savoyard Curate, in Rousseau's *Emile*, which belongs to this subject.

† Offic. Book I. Mr. *Wollaston*, in a *Note* to Sect. I. of his "Religion of Nature delineated," quotes this passage, but with less seeming approbation.

For though, in many cases, there is no great difficulty in discerning the path of duty, yet there are also many, in which, in order to a prompt and just decision, there is need of a judgment well-informed by instruction, and strengthened by repeated exertions. We should, therefore, as we have opportunity, make use of every means of improvement. As, in the application of reason to the discovery of a rule or criterion of virtue, we are not confined to any *one* rule, but are at liberty to adopt that, which is best suited to the nature of the case, or to our particular habits of thinking; so neither are we confined to the use of reason for the same purpose, to the exclusion of revelation. We may, nay (if we would perform our duty) we *must*, make use of both reason and revelation, and of all the methods, by which assistance is to be

derived

derived from either. To neglect either, when both are within our reach, is to incur, in a greater or less degree, the guilt of wilful ignorance of our duty; a crime, which, according to what has been already stated*, is of the same nature with that of the wilful transgression of it when known. In all cases, the foundation of morality is the will of God. Our knowledge of this will, as it respects human actions, is derived from the joint consideration of the divine attributes and the effects of human actions. In the case of the Heathens, the knowledge of the divine attributes and of the effects of human actions was left to be discovered by *reason* only. In the case of Jews and Christians, the knowledge of both, and more especially of the former, has been further discovered by *revelation*. So far

as

---

* See the beginning of this Chapter.

as morality depends on a knowledge of the divine attributes; that is, so far as the will of God, respecting the actions of men, can be deduced from those attributes, the morality of the Heathens was built on *natural* religion. To the same extent, the morality of Jews and Christians is; with equal propriety, and with as much regard to the rules of science, built on religion both *natural* and *revealed**. The consideration of the will of God, as

discovered

---

* If, indeed, there be any precepts in the religion of either Jews or Christians, which are of a purely *positive* nature, they must, as I have said, not coming within the province of morality as a science, rest on the *authority* of the particular revelation, which contains them. In the morality of the Jews, this observation is of extensive application; but it is the general method of the Christian revelation, as commanding a "rational service," to give, or at least to lead to, a *reason* for every thing, which it prescribes as a duty. It is, besides, to be remembered, that many duties prescribed in Scripture to both Jews and Christians, which are delivered in a positive *form*, are, in *reality*, obligatory in themselves, i.e. on grounds of reason.

discovered by revelation, is no more to be neglected, than the consideration of it as discovered or discoverable by reason: and, as it is evident, that, on the supposition of a revelation from heaven, it is our duty to attend to it; so is it equally evident, that it is our duty to examine, with candour and diligence, every religion, which has plausible pretensions to be a revelation.

It follows, from what has been remarked in this Chapter, that whoever draws up a system of morals comprehensive of Christian duties (as, it should seem, a system intended for the use of Christians ought to be) is bound to show, with respect to every such duty, whether it be obligatory in its own nature, or merely from positive command. In some cases, a further distinction may be necessary.

necessary. The *duty itself* may be obligatory in its own nature, and the *circumstances* of its performance matter of positive institution. When, for instance, we consider the general prevalence of *sacred days* and *sacred rites* among the Heathens, we are naturally led to think, that, though the *returns* and *mode of observing* the Christian Sabbath, as also the *number* and *mode of administering* the Christian Sacraments, be matters of positive institution, yet a *Sabbath* and *Sacraments* are obligatory in themselves, and rest on grounds of reason. Such distinctions, however, I repeat, are to be considered as affecting morality merely as a *science*, not as making any difference in the obligation we are under to obey its laws.

CHAP. IV.

ON THE *MOTIVE* TO VIRTUE.

HAVING seen what virtue *is*, and how we are to arrive at the *knowledge* of it, let us now consider the *inducement* to the practice of it. I am of opinion, that much confusion might have been avoided, if this part of the subject had always been considered separately. The *principle*, on which we perform an action, ought to be distinguished from the *motive*, by which we are actuated to its performance. It happens, indeed, that the same question may sometimes be answered, either by assigning the *principle* of action,

or

or by assigning the *motive*; and this circumstance may have contributed to the confusion, to which I refer. "Why do you keep your promise?" may be answered, by saying, "because I consider it as my duty to do so;" or by saying, "because I wish for the *rewards* (whether temporal* or eternal) arising from doing so." In the first answer, the *principle* of action is assigned; in the second, the *motive*. In both cases, the word *obligation* is sometimes used; but it can be used with propriety only in the first; obligation having reference to *duty* only, and not to *reward*. It is proper to say, "I am obliged to keep my promise, because it is my duty to do so;" but it is not proper to say, "I am obliged to keep my promise, because I am desirous of the rewards

---

* For instance, peace of conscience, the approbation of mankind, the various advantages of being credited.

rewards arising from doing so." In the latter case, it is more proper to say, "I am *induced* to keep my promise, by the rewards arising from doing so."

We may be incited to the practice of virtue by *various* motives, various at least *in form*, by any one or more of the rewards, which virtue holds out; but, as has been said, we can be virtuous only on *one* principle, that of voluntary obedience to the divine will. We act virtuously, whatever may be our *motive* of action, when we obey the will of God, and obey it with the intention of doing so. On the other hand, whatever may be the action itself, and whatever may be our motive to its performance, it is virtuous *only* as it is performed on a principle of duty. Different persons may perform the same actions, and be incited to the performance of them by the same *motives*, or by motives of the same *kind*, and yet perform them on very different *principles*. The hope of particular good, or the fear of particular evil, may incite us to do many things, on the principle of prudence, honour, pride, vanity, &c. which, however similar in themselves to actions performed on a principle of virtue, have no pretension to the name of virtue*. I do not deny, that the principle, on which we perform an action, and the motive, by which we are

---

* "It is possible to do good, and not be virtuous; for a man may be great in his actions, and little in his heart. Virtue is a quality much more rare than is generally imagined. It is proper, therefore, to be frugal of the words *virtue, humanity, patriotism,* and others of the same import. They ought to be mentioned only upon great occasions; for, by too frequent use, their meaning is weakened, and the qualities they describe brought into contempt." *Zimmermann* on *Solitude*. This passage furnishes a proof, among innumerable others, which might be mentioned, that common sense, without any reference to the principles, from which a truth is regularly deduced, is often directed by its influence.

are actuated to its performance, may refer to the same thing. What I contend for is, that, in acts of virtue, this is not the case, the one referring to the will of God, the other to the consequences of obeying it; and that it is not the nature of the motive, that determines whether any action *be* virtuous or not. By the providential disposition of things, which has place, and by which various inducements to action are held out to us, we are subjected to a great deal of *subordinate* discipline, by which, if we obey the dictates of our nature, we are brought nearer and nearer to the practice of virtue, and by which, in the mean time, many actions, immediately beneficial to ourselves and to others, are effected. For, in the present state of mankind, it is an evident error to suppose, that all beneficial actions, or even the greater part of them, are the effect

effect of virtue, or that they were intended to be so. We often act from motives only, without any regard to moral principle; and, in that case, the action, of whatever nature or tendency it may be in itself, if it properly admit of *any* moral denomination, does not admit of a *good* one. Actions, considered with respect to their moral quality, may be distinguished into *good*, *evil*, and *indifferent*; that is, actions commanded, actions forbidden, and actions neither commanded nor forbidden. To which class any particular action belongs, can only be determined by the reference, which the agent had in his mind to the will of God. It is possible, that he might have no such reference at all; and, though I do not say, that this would preserve him free from all moral *blame* (it being the general duty of a human being to have that reference in his

his mind) yet it certainly would exclude all juſt claim to *deſert,* and hinder his action from being *virtuous.*

Motive, then, is that, by which we are actuated to the purſuit of any object, and refers to the end we have in view. *Principle* is that, by which we are directed in the purſuit of our end or object, and refers to the mode of obtaining it*. A perſon

---

* Thus, when we ſpeak of a man's having no moral principle, we mean, that he purſues the object, which he has in view, by whatever means he happens to have in his power, without any regard to the dictates of virtue. For inſtance, all men, or at leaſt the generality of men, deſire to obtain riches and honours. The difference, with reſpect to this deſire, between thoſe, who are directed by the moral principle, and thoſe who are not, conſiſts in this; that, whereas the latter purſue their deſire by ſuch methods (ſomewhat different indeed in different perſons, according to their different meaſures of ſkill and prudence) as ſeem likely moſt eaſily or moſt ſurely to lead to the gratification of it, the former purſue it by ſuch methods only, as they deem to be agreeable to the will of God.

This may appear ſtill clearer from conſidering, that
motives

son may act on a wrong principle from right motives; or, as I would rather say, from *allowable* motives; because I do not think, that the idea of rectitude can be properly applied to motives. The converse of this is not true, both because motives cannot in themselves be wrong, and because a right principle, supposing it to exist, would prevent our acting from them, if they could be wrong*. Peace of mind,

---

motives and *principles* arise from a different *origin*. *Motives* are founded on the *propensitive* part of our nature, and arise from the inclinations, implanted in us, towards various external objects; or, in general, from the innate desire of happiness. *Principles*, on the other hand, are founded on the *reflective* or *reasoning* part of our nature, and arise from a regard to the *manner of gratifying* the desire of happiness; and the *moral principle*, in particular, founded on a consideration of the relation subsisting between God and ourselves, as created and dependent beings, arises from a regard to the manner, in which that desire may be gratified according to the will of God.

* For, though a right principle may consist with an error of the *understanding*, it cannot consist with any fault of the *will*.

mind, the approbation of good men, attainments in science, skill in arts, the enjoyments of the senses, may all be innocently aimed at; and the placing of happiness in one of them in preference to another, or the placing of it in any one thing to the exclusion of all others, is matter of wisdom or folly, rather than of virtue or vice. All the means of pleasure, whether of body or of mind, whether present or future, were appointed by the author of nature; and may all, if pursued on the principle of virtue, become the rewards of virtue. It is the peculiar danger, to which some modes of pleasure expose us of pursuing them exclusively, or of pursuing them without due regard to *principle*, which has brought them under the disrepute, not naturally belonging to them, of being considered as wrong in themselves. If any one should place

his

his happiness in obtaining the sovereign dominion of *Europe*, *Asia*, or *Africa*, or of all of them together, and should proceed to act on the romantick wish; yet, so long as he was restrained, by a right principle, from doing any thing inconsistent with the rules of virtue, or having the inclination to do it, in order to obtain the object of his wish, however unwisely we might justly deem him to act, we should hardly think, that he acted morally wrong. Nay, if any one should take delight in seeing, as a spectacle of awful sublimity, a thousand of his fellow-creatures mowed down by the fire of artillery, or blown up into the air by the explosion of a mine; yet, so long as he was unwilling to pursue any measures to obtain the gratification, which the sight might afford him, but such as virtue would strictly justify, we should not think him de-

serving

serving of moral blame, however little we might envy his taste.* This may seem to approach very nearly to that state of the *thoughts*, which is an undoubted offence against virtue. It is, however, a thing essentially different; for it is here supposed, that, if all the impediments to action, except the moral principle, were removed, no immoral action would still take place; and, though there may be virtues and vices of *thought*, where no correspondent action really takes place, yet it is always supposed, in either case, that, where the nature of the thought admits of it, action would follow, if some external impediment did not hinder it.†

But,

---

* It appears, from some of the dispatches of General *Buonaparte*, not to mention those of any other General, that this notion of happiness is not altogether so chimerical as, for the honour of human nature, we might otherwise be inclined to suppose.

† " The natural objects of affection," says Bishop *Butler*,

But, though motives cannot be right or wrong in themselves, some motives are, in their nature, much more favourable to virtue than others. Such motives may be conceived, as cannot easily consist with

Butler, " continue so. The necessaries, conveniencies, and pleasures of life, remain naturally desirable, though they cannot be obtained innocently; nay, though they cannot possibly be obtained at all. And, when the objects of any affection whatever cannot be obtained without unlawful means; but may be obtained by them: such affection, though its being excited, and its continuing some time in the mind, be as innocent as it is natural and necessary; yet cannot but be conceived to have a tendency to incline persons to venture upon such unlawful means; and therefore must be conceived as putting them in some *danger* of it." Analogy, Part I. Chap. 5. The Apostle indeed *(Rom.* 8. vii.) says, " The carnal mind is enmity against God; for it is not subject to the law of God, neither indeed can be;" which may seem to mean, that a regard to sensual gratifications of any kind, and in any degree, is evil in itself; yet it is evident, from the reason assigned by the Apostle, as well as from the nature of the thing, that such regard is only so far evil, as it leads us to disobey the rules of virtue, which God has prescribed to us. The mind, which is *engrossed* by carnal things, cannot obey the law, by which, for whatever reason, the enjoyment of carnal things is put under restriction.

with virtue. So that, though motives, suppoſing them known, cannot prove the exiſtence of virtue where it is (unleſs in the particular caſe, in which the reward aſpired to is ſuppoſed to be diſpenſed by the immediate act of God*,) they may, in many caſes, form a ſtrong preſumption againſt its exiſtence where it is not. It is, as we ſhall preſently have occaſion to obſerve more particularly, a neceſſary preliminary to virtuous practice, and *may* be a part of virtue itſelf, duly to regulate the affections; to place them on objects, according as they are adapted to promote happineſs; for our affections ought to be ſuch, as not only not to neceſſitate us to do wrong, but to aſſiſt us in doing right; and certain it is, according

to

---

* This caſe is excepted, becauſe it is ſcarcely poſſible to have reſpect, in our conduct, to the rewards, which we believe will be beſtowed by God *as* rewards of obedience to his will, without having reſpect alſo to that will itſelf.

to the maxim of our Saviour, that, "where our *treasure* is, there will our *heart* be also". The desire of happiness is a powerful propensity of the mind, which is always seeking for employment on one object or another*. If we set our affections on any thing, which cannot be obtained consistently with virtue, and are restrained by the principle of virtue from pursuing it, the consequence must be, that our mind is harrassed by contending desires, or reduced to an unnatural state of inactivity. I do not say, therefore, that the existence of such extravagant desires in the mind, as those just mentioned, would be likely to secure our happiness, or that they would not *endanger* our *virtue*. It is, undoubtedly, a matter of great importance,

---

* All men equally desire happiness, though different men have different notions of happiness, that is, place their happiness in different objects.

importance, that we should place our happiness in those things, which, from their nature, are most adapted to render it permanent, and which are most likely to be obtained by virtuous means. To the more particular confideration of this, however, we shall, as I have said, find occafion to return hereafter.

In oppofition to what has here been faid on the nature of *motives*, Dr. *Paley*, confidering them as conftituting obligation, fays, that "to be *obliged*, is to be urged by a violent motive, refulting from the command of another;" that "we can be obliged to nothing, but what we ourfelves are to gain or lofe fomething by;" and that "all obligation is nothing more than an *inducement* of fufficient ftrength." On the contrary, I am of opinion, that motive and obligation are

entirely

entirely independent of each other; that there might be an obligation to act, where there were no motives to act; and that there actually are motives to act, where there is no obligation. God, in his right over us as his creatures, might have made our duty to confift in fervices, to which we fhould have had no motive exclufively of pure command. That we are not, in fact, obliged to do any thing, to the doing of which we have not a reafonable motive, arifes, not from any neceffary relation between obligation and motive, but from the wifdom and goodnefs of God in not impofing that on us as a duty, to the performance of which we have not fuch a motive. The confideration of the poffibility of its being otherwife, added to that of the fact, that there are often motives, where there is no obligation, is, I think, fufficient to fhew, that

motive

motive and obligation are by no means *co-extensive*; and that, therefore, the one is not the conftituent of the other*.

"When

---

* So that, when we are inquiring, whether an action be virtuous or not, we have fomething more to do than to confider the *motive* of the agent. Having the fame motive, he may be led to very different actions, according as he is directed or not by a regard to the will of God, which is matter, not of *motive*, but of *principle*; and, even if his actions fhould be the fame, they would have different claims to be ranked among virtues, according as they were, or were not, the *refult* of that regard.

F. Malbranche, in his *Treatife of Morality,* agrees with me in diftinguifhing *virtue* itfelf from the *motive* to virtue. "After all, it is not properly the motive, which regulates the heart, but the love of order. Every motive is grounded on felf-love, on that invincible defire of being happy, which God continually infpires into us. A man, that burned with a defire of enjoying the prefence of God, to contemplate his perfections, and have a fhare in the felicity of the faints, would ftill deferve the punifhment of hell, if he had a difordered heart, and refufed to facrifice his predominant paffion to order. On the contrary, one, that was indifferent to eternal happinefs, if that were poffible, but in all other things was full of charity, &c. would be a juft man, and folidly virtuous; for, as I have already proved, true virtue, or a *conformity to the will of God*, confifts wholly in an habitual and ruling love of (*I* fhould

fay

"When I first turned my thoughts to moral speculations," says Dr. *Paley*, "an air of mystery seemed to hang over the whole subject; which arose, I believe, from hence, that I supposed, with many authors, whom I had read, that to be *obliged* to do a thing, was very different from being *induced* only to do it; and that the obligation to practise virtue, to do what is right, just, &c. was quite another thing, and of another kind, than the obligation, which a soldier is under to obey his officer, a servant his master, or any of the civil and ordinary obligations of human life." Though I would not be so harsh as to say, that Dr. *Paley* has left "confusion worse confounded"; yet I cannot help thinking, that, by supposing obligation and inducement to differ

---

say in acts of *obedience* to) "the eternal and divine law, the immutable order," The reader must not conclude, from this, that I accede to *all* the opinions of *F. Malbranche*.

fer in *degree* only, and not in *kind*, he has not contributed to clear up the myſtery, of which he complains. I think, that, when he "ſuppoſed, with many authors, whom he had read, that to be *obliged* to do a thing, was very different from being only *induced* to do it," he was juſtified by the nature of things, as well as by the authority of thoſe authors; but that, when he ſuppoſed the "obligation to practiſe virtue, to do what is right, juſt, &c. to be quite another thing, and of another kind, than the obligation, which a ſoldier is under to obey his officer, a ſervant his maſter, &c." he was juſtified by neither*. The latter part of the ſuppoſition

T

---

* Servants, obeying their maſters, "not with eye-ſervice, as men-pleaſers, but in ſingleneſs of heart, *fearing God*," and "doing the *will of God* from the heart," are able, and doubtleſs *ought*, to render the acts of their ſervitude ſo many acts of virtue; and the obſervation may be extended to the actions proper to every ſtation in life.

Thus,

sition is, by no means, a necessary consequence of the former; the cases referred to being only so many particular *instances* of virtue, to the performance of which there must, of course, be the same obligation, as to the practise of virtue in general. However, not to insist upon this, it is essential to my purpose to observe, that whatever may be determined with respect to obligation in general, *moral* obligation, as I hope has been sufficiently made out in Chap. I. results from God's will, and is constituted by God's command.

Dr.

Thus, our submission to civil authority, when it is rendered from a principle of obedience to the will of God, becomes the discharge of a moral duty. Accordingly, it is on this principle, that we are in Scripture exhorted to render that obedience. "Be subject," says the Apostle, "not only for *wrath*, but also for *conscience* sake"; not merely from fear of human punishment, but from a principle of duty to God. This point might be enlarged upon, especially in popular addresses, with very beneficial effect. St. *Paul*, in a most comprehensive passage to the purpose, furnishes an appropriate text. "Whether ye eat or drink, or whatsoever ye do, do all to the glory of God." See also Coloss. 3. xxiii.

Dr. *Paley* says, that " the difference, and the only difference, between an act of *prudence* and an act of *duty*, is, that, in the one case, we consider what we shall gain or lose in the present world; in the other case, we consider also what we shall gain or lose in the world to come." If, however, what I have said be just, it will follow, as a necessary consequence, that there is an *essential* difference between them; since, though both acts might proceed from the same *motive*, or from motives of the same *kind*, they are performed on different *principles*. Dr. *Paley*, admitting the impropriety of saying, that, " as I had made such a promise, it was *prudent* to perform it," thinks, that the impropriety arises from the reference here made to future rewards and punishments; whereas, if I mistake not, the impropriety arises from the circumstance, that

that the word prudence, in its common acceptation, does not include any reference to moral obligation, but merely to the proper means of obtaining any particular good, or of avoiding any particular evil. If there be no impropriety in saying, as I do not perceive there is, that 'men are *imprudent* in neglecting the means, by which their eternal state may be rendered as happy as possible;' it can hardly be thought, that the difference between prudence and virtue arises from the reference, which the one has to what we shall gain or lose in this world, and the other to what we shall gain or lose in the world to come. *Prudence*, in short, confining its regard to our advantage, whatever it may be supposed to be, takes no other notice of the means, by which it is to be obtained, than as they are more or less adapted to obtain it; and is, indeed,

indeed, nothing else than the application of wisdom to our own advantage in a particular case. *Virtue*, on the other hand, forbids us to pursue any end, except in one particular way. Undoubtedly, it is the highest *instance* of prudence, to apply ourselves to the study and the practice of virtue; but this does not make prudence and virtue to be the same*. Let us, however, proceed to the more immediate consideration of the motive to virtue.

I do not hesitate to pronounce, that the *end* of virtue is the happiness of individuals†. This happiness may consist in

various

---

* The near connection between *wisdom* and *virtue* has sometimes occasioned them to be used promiscuously one for the other. In the Scriptures, and in the writings of Philosophers, virtue is often called wisdom; but then this is done *rhetorically*, rather than *philosophically*; and it is thus, if I mistake not, that wisdom, or that branch of wisdom, which we call prudence, is to be considered as virtue.

† At first sight, this may seem inconsistent with saying,

as

various particulars, but chiefly in the exaltation of character; and this exaltation is to be effected by the repetition of acts of obedience to the divine will, until a *habit* of obedience to that will is formed, and that likeness to God, of which the particular beings, from their nature and constitution, are capable, is perfected in them. This, if I mistake not, is the end of all human virtue, from the duty of *Adam* in paradise, which consisted in the observance of a single precept, to the duty of persons in the most complicated situations of life. In the mean time, whatever is the character of men, at any stage of their progress towards perfection, there is a proper happiness belonging to it, the

consideration

---

as I have said in the second Chapter, that the *end* of virtue is the perfection, or however the *improvement*, of the moral character. The inconsistency, however, is only in *appearance*. Perfection or improvement of character is an end, in order to one still more remote; that is, the *happiness* of the perfected or improved being.

consideration of which is not to be neglected. It hence follows, that private happiness is the proper *motive* to virtue. For though, in fact, the *end*, which God designed in the actions of men, is not always the *motive* to the agent; yet we may safely affirm, that, when known, it *ought* to be so*. That *all* motives are

not

---

* The author of the "Examination of the leading principle of the new system of morals," to whom I have already referred with *general* commendation, says, " I may venture to affirm, that there is no single instance, no, not the minutest, in the whole moral economy of man, in which the *end* to be attained, is the *motive* appointed to attain it. Let us take the most familiar cases, that can occur. The end of eating and drinking is the support of our bodies; do we eat and drink for that purpose? The end of the union of the sexes is the propagation of the species; do we unite with that view? The end of parental affection is the preservation of helpless infancy; do we love our children on that account?" But we may observe, with respect to each of these instances, and others of the like kind, that what is here assigned as the end, is not the *whole* of the end appointed. There is every reason to suppose, that the pleasure of the agent was also an end in view, though intended as a means to a still further end. With respect to the first instance, the manner, in which, in many places of Scripture,

not *inconsistent* with the moral principle, will appear from considering the effect of motives

ture, the idea of self-gratification is connected with that of eating and drinking, shows, that there at least the immediate pleasure of the individual is considered as part of the end intended. With respect to the second instance also, we have Scriptural authority for supposing, that part at least of the appointed end was the immediate benefit of the individual agents; that is, the "mutual society, help, and comfort, that the one ought to have of the other, both in prosperity and adversity;" for we are in Scripture expressly told, that the "Lord God said, It is not good, that the man should be *alone*: I will make him an help meet for him."

Besides, if what is here assigned as the end, make, in fact, no part of our motive, in the instances referred to; will any one deny, that it ought to do so? or affirm, that there is any reason *against* its doing so? By reasoning from the motive in *fact* to the motive *appointed*, we may easily draw an erroneous conclusion. From facts, which are the pure result of natural operations, we may conclude with certainty (or, however, with high probability) respecting the intentions of nature; but not so from those, which depend, whether in substance or form, on the arbitrary customs or opinions of men. Let us take another instance or two. The *end* of civil society is *mutual protection and comfort*. Do not men unite, or continue united, in civil society for that purpose? The *end* of military establishments is the *defence of the state*. The *actual motive* for entering into military service is, it must be owned, often different from this; often that of *rank*, *pecuniary profit*, or

both.

motives in the production of any particular action. In a case of distress, we may afford relief from a sentiment of compassion, from a sense of duty, or from the expectation of reward. If we are led to afford relief merely from the sentiment of *compassion*, the action is not, strictly speaking, *virtue*; but something *less*, or something *more*. For, if the sentiment of compassion, by which we are actuated, be the mere effect of the moral sense, as implanted

---

both. These are *allowable* motives; but who will deny, that the motive of protecting the state is a more honourable one? who will deny, that, under many circumstances, men *ought* to enter into military service with the sole view of protecting the state? Since, however, as I have shewn, (or endeavoured to show) virtue does not depend on motives, all that is necessary for my purpose is, that the motive *may* be the same as the appointed end; that there is no moral objection *against* it; and it cannot, I think, be pretended that there is.

Since the above was written, the Author of the "Examination, &c." in a second edition of his work, has avowed himself to be my learned and ingenious friend, *Thomas Green*, Esq. of *Ipswich*.

implanted by nature, the action resulting from it implies no *volition*, and is consequently deficient in an essential part of virtue. If it be the effect of that sense improved by repeated acts of virtue, so as to have become the habit of the mind, it is rather an expression of that godlike disposition, which it is the intention of virtue to produce, than a particular act of virtue. It is in neither of these ways, however, that men are generally led to afford relief in cases of distress. For we are to consider, that, between the feelings of compassion for distress, and the act of the mind, by which we are determined to relieve it, various considerations often intervene. In instances of fancied misery, indeed, such as are represented to us in epic, or dramatic poetry, or in those, which are real, but in which we have no immediate concern, the sentiment of compassion

passion does all that is requisite, and leaves no room for the exertion of other powers. Perceiving no impediments in the way, we go on, in imagination, to relieve the misery we compassionate, just as we should endeavour to remove a suffering of our own. But, in real life, where the act of relieving is likely to occasion some immediate inconvenience to ourselves, the case is different. There, the sentiment of compassion is often felt, and no effort made to relieve the misery, by which compassion is excited. It sometimes happens, indeed, that those, who most warmly compassionate scenes of fancied misery, are most hard-hearted in cases of real distress. For, though the sentiment of compassion should clearly *direct* to what is right, it may still have no influence in *inducing* us to do it; that is, it may be a sufficient *rule* of virtue, when it is not

effectual

effectual as a *motive*. It is necessary, in the generality of men, that the consideration of the inconvenience, which they would incur by relieving real distress, should be overcome by other considerations of a *positive* nature. If the sole consideration, which calls us into action, is that of the return, which is likely to be made us by the person relieved, or of the credit and reputation, which we shall obtain in the estimation of others, I need not say, that all idea of *virtue* is out of the question. Here, the motive directs the principle; and the principle is nothing more than a regard to the manner, by which the particular object in view may most effectually be obtained. Accordingly, our exertions in the action itself will be regulated by the apparent probability of obtaining that object. But, if the determination of the mind to afford relief

be

be made from considerations of duty, from a regard to the will of God, the action resulting from it is a virtuous one, even though we have been previously determined to act virtuously by the advantages of doing so*. For it is sufficient to constitute the virtue of any particular action, that the first principle of its performance be a sense of duty, though we have received the general determination to act on that principle from considerations

---

* There is an essential difference between considering how the mind is determined to the practice of virtue in *general*, and how it is determined to act so or so in *particular instances*. The advantages, which God has annexed to the practice of virtue, may very properly be our motive to the first; but, in particular actions, there can be no virtue, unless the principle of obedience to the divine will precede all regard to motives. At the time of action, a virtuous man does not inquire what he shall gain by acting so or so, but what is the line of duty. Indeed, the advantages to be expected from particular actions would form very inadequate motives to right conduct: for though, by the appointment of God, our duty and our interest coincide on *the whole*, they do not coincide in every *particular instance*.

tions of advantage to ourselves. It will easily be seen, that the acting on a principle thus constituted answers the great purpose of virtue, the exercise of our obedience to the will of God, and the consequent perfecting or improving of our nature; and that, moreover, it secures to our conduct all the stability, which it could derive from our acting on the most disinterested considerations, and without reference to any motives at all. Undoubtedly, our duty is simply, and without regard to any thing extraneous, to obey the will of God; but, since it has pleased God, by implanting in us the desire of happiness, to make way for the super-addition of *motives*; they cannot in themselves be inconsistent with our duty; nor can an action be rendered otherwise than virtuous, merely by our having reference to that consideration, by which it was the intention

intention of God, that we should be impelled to its performance*.

It appears, from what has been already said, that Dr. *Paley* also considers the happiness of the individual to be the motive to virtue; but that he confines it to the happiness of the *life to come*. Are there, then, we may ask, no *present* rewards of virtue? and may not these be the proper inducements to virtuous practice? I am of opinion, that the rewards of virtue, however they may occasionally be

---

* *Adam* was furnished with a motive to obedience; namely, the dread of punishment threatened to disobedience; yet his obedience, had he persevered in it, would have been *virtue*. Whether it would have been *more* virtuous to persevere in his obedience, without the superaddition of such a motive, it would be idle to inquire. It pleased God to super-add that motive; and we may thence conclude, that, in the case of human beings, surrounded as they are with temptations to depart from their duty, the assistance of motives is necessary to keep them steady in the practice of it.

be intercepted, were intended to be enjoyed by man in every stage of his existence; and that, therefore, a regard to those, which are of a temporal nature only, so far from being inconsistent with virtue, is one of the proper and appointed incentives to virtue. Mr. *Hume* having erroneously made the motive to virtue to be *temporal happiness*, Dr. *Paley*, as if to correct the error, makes it to be *everlasting happiness*; whereas, if I mistake not, both opinions are equally erroneous; though certainly, with respect to its practical effects, that of Mr. *Hume* is much more dangerously so. The motive, which Mr. *Hume* assigns, is indeed *insufficient*; but it is not therefore *unnecessary*, and it ought not to be rejected. Naturally, and according to the tendency of things, virtue has the "rewards of the life, that now is, as well as of that, which is to come."

come." With particular exceptions we are not now concerned. In the different stages of our existence, different *notions* of happiness will, of course, be formed by us; and, as I have admitted, it is important, that they at all times be such, as are suitable to our nature, and such as may most effectually lead us to the practise of virtue: but it is not necessary, in order to render our conduct virtuous, that it be the effect of a regard to our happiness by one thing rather than by another, in one period of our existence rather than in another. As our character improves in other respects, it will improve in estimating things according to their real value, their competency to promote our permanent happiness. Accordingly, our affection for what can afford us only immediate and momentary gratification will gradually diminish. But if, informed of no

existence

existence beyond the present life, we yet act in obedience to the will of God, our having respect only to present happiness will not hinder us from being truly virtuous. We certainly shall not be required to act with a regard to that, of which we are innocently ignorant.

Dr. *Paley*, after stating the question, ' will there be, after this life, any distribution of rewards and punishments?' considers an affirmative reply to it as a necessary support of his system; so that, according to that system, the obligation to morality can extend to those only, who do so answer it. But, surely, under whatever disadvantages, with respect to motives, the want of belief in a future state might place men, virtue was always *obligatory* on them, and there were always inducements to practise virtue,

whether

whether they had that belief or not. Accordingly, Dr. *Paley* admits, that those, who would establish a system of morality independent of a future state, must look out for an idea of moral obligation different from that, which he has given; a concession, which sufficiently shows the necessity of so looking out; for an idea of virtue, which excuses the heathens from the obligation of virtue, and which, as has been already observed,* excludes them from the capacity of acting virtuously, will not easily be admitted as a just one. The truth is, Dr. *Paley* makes morality to depend too much on the credibility of the Christian revelation. The Christian revelation, no doubt, is to be highly valued, both for instructing us more fully in moral duties, and for increasing

---

* See what was said, in Chap. I. on Dr. *Paley's Definition* of Virtue.

creasing and strengthening the motives to their observance; but as, without any reference to Christianity, virtue may be shown to be obligatory, so also, independently of that, may it be shown to have very powerful inducements to its practice. Of this the third book of *Cicero's Offices*, in which he shows the co-incidence of virtue with temporal advantages, is a sufficient proof and illustration. But let us now consider the case of heathen virtues more distinctly.

It is an opinion, which has been entertained by many, that those actions of the heathens, which seem to have the fairest pretension to be called virtues, and even *heroic* virtues, were no more, in reality, than so many *splendid crimes*. Yet, to the continence of Scipio Africanus, the probity of *Aristides* and *Fabricius*,

the

the magnanimity of the *Decii* and *Regulus*, &c. it can hardly be thought reasonable not to allow *all* the excellence, of which human actions are capable. Whatever, in these and similar instances, may be determined respecting the *whole character* of the agents; it seems strange to doubt whether the particular actions, which have obtained the approbation of all succeeding ages, were possessed of the quality, which alone can render actions, considered abstractedly from their immediate effects, deserving of approbation. Still less reasonable will it be, perhaps, in the estimation of some, to deny the praise of virtue to thousands of persons, unnamed in the page of history, who, in the retired walks of private life, without the incitement of glory, quietly performed the numerous and sometimes painful duties of their several stations. Who can

overlook

overlook the pretensions to moral merit, at least in parts of their conduct, of *Plato, Aristotle, Cicero, Epictetus,* &c.? Above all, who does not revere the seemingly general and perfect virtue of *Socrates?* In what degree, indeed, any individuals among the heathens were virtuous, or whether, in fact, they were virtuous at all, cannot with certainty be determined; because it would be necessary, in order to determine either, previously to know, what can be known only by him, who is able to search the heart, on what *principle* they acted. I readily admit, that their conduct was only so far virtuous, as it was designed obedience to the divine will. Be the fact, however, as it may, I contend, that, if the actions, to which the praise of virtue has been so generally attributed, were not virtues, it was not owing to the nature of the *motives,* by

which

which the performers of them were actuated. It will, indeed, hardly be thought, when the matter is confidered feparately from other circumftances, that the performance of an action for the fake of eternal happinefs, and the performance of the fame action for the fake of temporal happinefs, can conftitute the difference between virtue and the want of it. Though the heathens might be incited to action by motives, which we fhould not now judge to be the *beft*, the moft likely to render them conftant and uniform in virtue, they might be incited by fuch, as (to fpeak the common language about motives) in their fituation were *allowable* ones; and, whatever were their motives, they might, as has been explained, act on a right *principle*. Though they might feek their own happinefs, in the acquifition of fome temporal good,

good, they might still seek it in those ways, in which they conceived it was the will of the Deity to confer it. Who can doubt, that the conduct of *Scipio*, in the instance referred to, was agreeable to the will of God? who can deny, that *Scipio* pursued it, *knowing* it to be so? I do not say, that this conception alone rendered *any* action, which they might perform in consequence of it, a virtuous action; but that, so long as it existed, the circumstance of their being incited to action by motives, which were confined to *temporal* advantages only, did not hinder their actions from being truly virtuous. I have already said, that an action, in order to be virtuous, must not only be *supposed* by the agent to be an act of obedience to the divine will, but that it must also actually *be* so; that, taking into consideration the situation of the agents, which we cannot suppose

suppose God not to do, virtue is *real* as well as *designed* obedience to the will of God. That there is, however, some difference in the duty of man, at different stages of his progress in improvement, cannot well be doubted. God, it is true, is always the same; but man, varying with the situation, in which he happens to be placed, is very different at the different periods of his civilization. It cannot, therefore, be supposed, that his duties, whether to God, his neighbour, or himself, are always exactly the same; or that God requires from him, under the different dispensations of nature, law, and grace, the same performances*. It was

the

---

* In *all* cases, as I have repeatedly observed, the foundation of morality is the will of God. In the case of heathens, this will is left to be discovered by *reason* only: consequently, the morality of heathens is built on *natural religion*. In the case of Jews and Christians, the will of God is further discovered by *revelation:* consequently, the

morality

the duty of the Jews to observe all the particulars of the Mosaic ritual; that is, it was the *real* will of God, that they should do so. But this cannot be said, with respect to any other people than the Jews, nor, at the present period, with respect to them. As, therefore, it may be contended, in opposition to Mr. *Hume*, that the rewards and punishments of futurity are proper motives to virtue, being the appointment of God for that purpose; so may it also be contended, in opposition to Dr. *Paley*, that present good and evil, the appointment of God for the same purpose, are motives of the same sort, however inferior in degree.

If, in supposed conformity to the sense of the 13th Article of our national Church,

it

---

morality of Jews and Christians is built on religion both *natural* and *revealed*.

it be alledged, that the heathens could not act virtuously, or acceptably to God, without the "grace of Christ, and the inspiration of his Spirit," it may be answered, that though, from the circumstances of their situation, the heathens could not have actual "*faith* in Christ;" yet we have no authority for asserting, that the grace, which is here supposed necessary to render actions pleasing to God, was not bestowed on many, before the appearance of Christ on earth.* All that

---

* On this subject, I not unwillingly lead the mind of the reader to the Article of our Church, which relates to it; both because I think, that the consideration of the Article may throw light on the subject, and that what is here said may tend to confirm the sense, in which, as I think, the Article itself ought to be understood. It will easily be seen, that the general sense of it is at least reconcileable with what I have all along insisted on; namely, that actions, of whatever nature or tendency they may be in themselves, are not to be esteemed virtuous, unless they are done in known or supposed obedience to the will of God. Those, who wish for a fuller discussion of the Article,

that can be justly expected of men is, that they should live according to the law,

ticle, may consult the judicious explanation and comment of Dr. *Hey*, in his *Norrisian Lectures*.

F. *Malbranche*, whom I have quoted before, admits the justness of the opinion, that grace, sufficient to enable men to act virtuously, was bestowed before the coming of Christ. Though the *whole* of the passage, in which this appears, is not appropriate to the present subject, I transcribe it as curious and important. "There are several reasons, why the law (the *Mosaic* law) did not promise the true blessings; but one of the chief is, that, since this sort of enjoyments cannot be the object of concupiscence, the knowledge and worship of the true God would have been soon lost among the Jews, and that chosen people reduced to a handful of men, *belonging to Christ, and sanctified in every age by inward grace*. But it was necessary, that the knowledge of the true God should be preserved with some lustre among the Jews, a prophetical people, and an unexceptionable witness of the truths of religion, in spite of all the power and artifices of the prince of this world, until, at length, the only-begotten Son of God, for and by whom all things were made, should come down from heaven, to change the face of things over all the earth, and to open the surprizing and wonderful scene of God's conduct." Still more directly to the purpose does Archbishop *Tillotson*, speaking of *Socrates*, *Epictetus*, *Antoninus*, &c. allow, " that they were not wholly destitute of an inward principle of goodness." " For though," says that sensible and amiable Divine,

law, under which they are placed; and God, we may be assured, always does what is right. A preparation of mind for the reception of Christianity, seems all that is essentially necessary, in order to render men capable of many of its benefits. Now, the general prevalence of expiatory sacrifices is a sufficient evidence, that the heathens were not without a sense of the *want* of a Redeemer; and this, perhaps, was all the preparation of mind, which the situation of the heathens admitted. Who can doubt, that *Socrates*, in the frame and disposition of his mind, was prepared for the reception of Christianity? Indeed, it can scarcely be doubted, that

---

Divine, " they had not that powerful grace and assistance of God's Holy Spirit, which is promised and afforded to all sincere Christians, (as neither had the Jews, who were the peculiar people of God, and in covenant with him) yet it is very credible, that such persons were under a special care and providence of God, and not wholly destitute of *divine assistance.*" Sermon 209.

that very many of the heathens were thus prepared for its reception; would actually have received it, if it had been preached to them. That it was not preached to them, was no *fault* in them; and we cannot suppose, that they would, on that account, be excluded from such an important benefit of the mediatorial scheme, as to be left under the incapacity of improving their dispositions by the practice of virtue, by the performance of actions, which might render them still fitter objects of God's mercy and favour*. I believe, that, in fact, very *many* of the splendid deeds of the heathens were far from being virtues; not, however, because they were not performed on Christian principles, or suggested by Christian motives,

---

* I do not mean to deny, that those, to whom Christianity is actually made known, have not many advantages over others. To some of these advantages, indeed, we shall presently have occasion to refer.

motives, which, from the situation of the heathens, was impossible; but because they were not performed on that principle of obedience to the will of God, of which the actions even of heathens were capable. The Christian doctrine, that *good works* (i.e. works beneficial to men) avail nothing to the attainment of *salvation* (i.e. of the effects, whatever they might be, of God's favour) unless they come of *faith*, was always true: for this, allowing for the change of circumstances, is the same as saying, that no action, which is not performed in intended obedience to the will of God, is truly *virtuous*, in whatever degree it may promote the benefit of mankind.

Notwithstanding, then, the apprehensions of those, who think, that, by admitting the happiness of the agent as

the

the motive to virtue, we make virtue to be too *selfish* a thing*; or that, by admitting

---

* The author of the *Characteristics* argues against Christianity on the ground, that it attempts to promote the practice of virtue by threats and promises of *any* sort; alledging, that "neither the fear of future punishment, nor the hope of future reward, can possibly be called good affections, or such as are the acknowledged springs and sources of actions truly good;" and further, that "this fear, or this hope cannot *consist* in reality with virtue or goodness." I quote from a quotation of the passage in Dr. *Watts' Improvement of the mind*, Part I. Chap. 10. "Doth *Job* fear God for *nought?*" was indeed alledged by Satan, as an argument against the integrity of *Job*. This implied, however, not only that *Job* was encouraged to perseverance in virtue by the hope of reward, but that his virtue was the mere result of that hope, that he acted entirely from *motives*. The event showed how much Satan was mistaken in his estimate of *Job*'s character, and that *Job* served God from a principle of duty. Had Lord *Shaftesbury* attended to the distinction, which I have pointed out, and which, if I mistake not, is founded in the nature of things, between the *principle* and the *motive* to virtue, he probably would not have thought his objection of any weight. The virtue of *Job* was real virtue, notwithstanding the hope, by which he was supported, that God would restore him to temporal prosperity; and the virtue of Christians may be real virtue, notwithstanding the hope, by which they are encouraged, that God will confer on them

admitting any other happiness, than what is future and eternal, as the motive, we detract them eternal happiness. The misfortune of Lord *Shaftesbury* seems to have been, what indeed, if I mistake not, is the case of most other conscientious arguers against the truth of Christianity, that, having a great many sublime moral ideas in his head, which he contemplated with sincere and ardent admiration, he did not know how to reduce them to a right order, or to trace their relation and connection. From this accusation (if it may not rather be called an *apology*) I do not except Mr. *Hume*, notwithstanding the *appearance*, in many of his writings, of discriminate conception, and studied propriety of arrangement. In justification of this, I need only refer to the refutation of his *Essay on Miracles* by the late Dr. *Adams*.

It is with great pleasure, that I am now (April 1799) able to refer the reader to another satisfactory refutation of Mr. *Hume*'s Essay on Miracles, entitled, "The credibility of Christianity vindicated, in answer to Mr. *Hume*'s objections; in two Discourses preached before the University of *Cambridge*, by the Rev. S. *Vince*, A.M. F.R.S. Plumian Professor of Astronomy and Experimental Philosophy:" a publication peculiarly valuable, as furnishing a fresh and striking proof, that the habitual employment of the mind in the depths of mathematical research does not *always* indispose it for the relish and reception of that kind and degree of evidence, on which the truth of revelation rests; thus strongly tending to eradicate the unfounded notion, alike prejudicial to science as to religion, that the study of the mathematics is necessarily unfavourable to the belief of revelation.

detract from the dignity of virtue, we may, I think, safely conclude, that the proper and appointed motive to virtue is, *the general happiness of the agent.* Both objections, indeed, are in great measure obviated by the idea, with which I set out; by separating the motive to virtue from virtue itself, and making nothing essential to virtue but voluntary obedience to the will of God. Those, who have well considered human nature, will see but little ground to expect, that, independently of the hope of reward and the fear of punishment, virtue will be at all practised, or practised in any considerable degree. It is worthy of remark, that the Scriptures do not encourage the idea of such a *disinterested* virtue, as some, who acknowledge the authority of the Scriptures, have thought it necessary to recommend. "Without faith," we are told,

told, "it is impossible to please God." And why? "Because he, that cometh to God" (in order, that is, to please him, by the practice of virtue) "must believe, that he is, and that he is a *rewarder* of them, who diligently seek him." The reward in view, indeed, the particular object of desire, is different, according to men's different notions of happiness; but, in all,

"*Self-love*, the spring of action, moves the soul."

In proportion, however, as the moral principle increases in strength, there is the less need of motives, especially of those motives, which are founded on immediate and temporal advantages; and there is a state of mind, to which we have the ability of attaining, or at least of approaching nearer and nearer, which, without any external impulse, will incline us to a spontaneous obedience to the divine will; in which, to

use

use the figure of our Saviour concerning himself, it will be our *meat and drink* to do the will of our heavenly Father; the state, to which St. *John* seems to refer, when he speaks of that " perfect love, which casteth out," and consisteth not with "fear*." But this, if I mistake not, is rather the *effect* of virtuous practice, than virtuous practice itself. This, as I have already said,† is that perfection of our nature, which it is the design of virtue gradually to produce; and which, in proportion as it is produced, delivers us from the necessity of the discipline, to which, as men, we are at first wisely subjected, and exalts us to the state and condition of Angels§. When this goodness of disposition

---

* I. John, iv. 18. † See end of Chap. II.

§ In Scripture, the disposition thus produced is called *holiness*. The Angels are stiled *holy*. "Without *holiness*," it is said, "no man shall see the Lord." Thus, then, the practice of *virtue*, as it respects the agent, leads to *holiness*.

position is completely attained, and the habit of obedience to the divine will wrought into the constitution of the mind, the necessity of external motives ceases; then is the agent happy from himself, and in the contemplation, nay in the performance, of his own actions; then, and (as I think) *only* then, may virtue truly be said, if virtue it can then be called, to be its *own reward*.

It may be proper here to take notice of an opinion, which has sometimes been entertained to the disparagement of virtue, that the performance of an act of beneficence from *sentiment* or *feeling*, is to be preferred to the performance of the same act from considerations of duty. To the opinion itself I have nothing to object. I readily admit, that good actions, which flow spontaneously from the disposition of the mind, are more amiable than those, which are performed on a principle of virtue. But I enter my protest against that application of the opinion, which has now been referred to; against setting the principle of virtue in opposition to the effect, which virtue is intended to produce. It should be recollected, that these spontaneous acts of goodness are so many instances, in which the discipline of virtue has had "its perfect work," or in which, from the happy conformation of the mind by nature, that discipline was not necessary. That it would not be safe to trust to nature alone for bestowing on *all* persons a disposition to right conduct in any particular point, or for bestowing on *any* a disposition to right conduct in *every* point, at least a disposition strong enough to overcome the impediments to it, which must necessarily

sarily be encountered, I need only appeal to the experience of each individual to evince. This testimony, therefore, to the charms of a virtuous frame and disposition of mind, ought, as an earnest of the happy fruits of virtue, to be an argument for its diligent cultivation. Far from interpreting the instances, in which such a disposition is exerted, to the prejudice of virtue, we should consider them as similar in their nature to virtue herself; as (to speak *rhetorically*) so many features of virtue in that form, in which, if she fully displayed herself to mortals, she would, it has been said, command their lasting admiration and love*.

But,

---

* "Formam quidem ipsam, Marce fili, et tanquam faciem honesti vides; quæ, si oculis cerneretur, mirabiles amores (ut ait *Plato*) excitaret sapientiæ." *Cicero* de Off. Lib. i. 5. Another instance, by the way, in which wisdom and virtue are considered as synonymous.

But, though happiness is the "end and aim of our being," and, consequently, the desire of happiness, whether present or future, temporal or eternal, the proper motive to virtue, it is yet very important to inquire in what particulars happiness may most justly be considered to consist. Though all the incitements to virtue may be referred to *self-love*, they are of very different efficacy in promoting the practice of virtue. It is necessary, in order to secure the practice of it in the greatest degree possible, that we confine our idea of happiness to the things, of which virtue leads to the most certain possession, and which are sources of the most lasting enjoyments; and, in proportion as we attain to that idea, our motive to virtue will be strengthened and improved. Without due care in this respect, we may easily place our affections on objects, which,

after

after carrying us certain lengths in the road of virtue, will afford us no assistance in a further progress. It cannot, I think, be denied, that the desire of honourable distinction among men, whether by the possession of riches, authority, or fame, is often, what it was doubtless intended to be, the incitement to virtuous pursuits (for the desire of such distinction is not, as I trust I have evinced, *inconsistent* with our acting in obedience to the will of God, however it may sometimes interfere with our doing so) yet disappointment or satiety may so diminish the relish for these, and similar possessions, as to leave him, who is actuated by no other motives, destitute of all incitements to future exertion. The importance, indeed, of having just conceptions of human happiness, or at least of attaining to a knowledge of the things, which principally contribute to

happiness,

happiness, is sufficiently evident*. It is well known how much the subject has engaged the attention of moralists of all ages. Among the ancients, an inquiry into the nature of the *summum bonum*, which, according to *Cicero, continet philosophiam*, generally formed the groundwork of their moral systems; and the different opinions, which different sects of philosophers held respecting it, were considered as one of their chief characteristics. That their search was ineffectual, appears from

---

* A distinction ought to be made between a *state* of happiness, as an *end*, and the *constituents* of happiness, as an *efficient cause*. Dr. *Paley*, in his Chapter on happiness, for want of noticing this distinction, has incurred an *apparent* inconsistency. For instance, among the things, in which he reckons happiness *not to consist*, he mentions the "pleasures of music, painting, architecture, gardening, &c." yet afterwards, among the things, in which happiness *does consist*, he enumerates the "building of a house, the laying out of a garden, the digging of a fish-pond, &c." It is evident, however, on consideration, that, in the first case, he must intend to speak of these pleasures as an *end*, and as being the *state* of happiness; in the second, as part of the *efficient cause*, and as *contributing* towards that state.

from this single circumstance, that various opinions concerning it were maintained by men of nearly equal ability and authority. For, even if one of these opinions had been true; yet, while sufficient evidence of its truth was wanting, few would admit it as a motive of conduct. In this case, uncertainty is nearly the same with total ignorance. So long as almost every notion of happiness, which it is possible to conceive, was sheltered by the patronage of a respectable name, and supported by a show of argument, it was easy for each one to persuade himself, that, in following his own inclination, he was pursuing the dictates of reason. Whoever wishes to have some idea of these opinions, may consult the entertaining account given of them by *Cicero*, in his books *de finibus bonorum et malorum*; and he will probably be convinced, at the same time,

time, how deficient and unsatisfactory they all were*. On the same subject, he may consult also, with still more advantage, the sacred book of *Ecclesiastes*, the best, perhaps, of all the systems of morality, which are not indebted to the Christian revelation, even independently of the *authority*, which it derives from inspiration. *Solomon's* inquiry plainly shows, what no inquiries of the heathen philosophers seem to have done, that though every thing, which God has provided for the use of man, is good in its proper measure and season; yet that, properly speaking, there is nothing earthly,

---

* *Cicero*, however, takes notice of those opinions only, which were of most distinguished eminence. "In the time of *Varro*" (who was co-temporary with *Cicero*) "the different opinions on moral subjects were so extravagantly multiplied, that, in his book of philosophy (see August. de civ. Dei, l. xix. c. 1.) he reckons up two hundred and eighty-eight several opinions concerning the *summum bonum* only." *Baker*'s Reflections upon Learning, Chap. 6.

ly, which is man's *supreme* or *only* good; and that he, who thinks there is, will be in perpetual danger of falling into the apathy of the Stoics, or into the dissoluteness of the Epicureans*. It is observable also, that *Solomon*, though he was not able to satisfy himself, nor consequently his readers, respecting what is the *chief good*, deduces from his inquiry a just account of human virtue. "Let us hear," says he, "the conclusion of the whole matter: Fear God, and keep his commandments;

---

* It is curious to observe the agreement and difference between *Solomon* and the Stoics, in their ideas of *wisdom*. According to both, the perfectly *wise* man (to use the technical term) is perfectly *virtuous*, and the characteristic of the *fool* is *vice*. They differ, however, in this, that whereas the wise man of *Solomon* enjoys all pleasures, which are not inconsistent with virtue, the wise man of the Stoics, not making a distinction of things according to their nature, and the intention of God in bestowing them, denies himself many innocent enjoyments. The one may be considered as placed in a paradise, where the fruit of one tree only is forbidden; the other in a paradise, where all the products are forbidden fruit.

mandments; for this is the whole duty of man." The meaning of which seems to be, that the virtue of human beings consists in attaining to a knowledge of God, as their creator and preserver, and in living in obedience to his will.

The most important use, however, which we can now make of these inquiries, is, to deduce from them a conviction of the obligations, which morality owes in this matter to revelation. We have already noticed the advantages, which are derived from revelation in general, as a *teacher* of moral duties. Those, which are derived from it, and particularly from the Christian revelation, with respect to *motives*, are equally entitled to our attention and gratitude. In the opinion of some, indeed, it is the distinguishing character of revelation, not that it more

fully

fully makes *known* the will of God, but that it furnishes more powerful motives to *perform* it. Be this as it may, it is sufficiently evident, from the investigations referred to, how greatly reason was at a loss to fix upon those inducements to the practice of virtue, which we now know to be the most powerful, or to fix upon any with that steadiness, which was necessary to give them due effect. The Christian revelation, by unfolding to us the nature and design of our present situation, by setting forth this life as a state of discipline and probation for a future and immortal one, in which we shall be rewarded or punished according to our behaviour here, or in which our happiness or misery will depend upon the habits and dispositions contracted here, opens topics of persuasion to the practice of what it enjoins, which before could either not be urged

urged at all, or not urged with any sensible effect. The motives to virtue, which reason could furnish, were chiefly confined to the present advantages, with which the practice of virtue is attended. For, though it cannot be said, that a future life was entirely unknown, or disbelieved, by the ancient heathens; there is no evidence of its being so known and believed, as to have much influence on their conduct. Besides, granting the probability of a *future life* to be discoverable by reason, it may still be contended, that the *rewards* of eternity, as we now understand them, being the free gift of God through Christ, could not be known but by revelation. The heathens, unacquainted with the *destination* of man, were but ill qualified to reason on the nature of his situation here. If they considered this life as the whole of their existence,

istence, and had no respect to it as a state of probation and preparation for another, it was natural for them to esteem, as the greatest good, the object most suited to their inclinations. And this being in fact the case, it would as naturally follow, that the leader of each sect would gain to his opinion, however erroneous it might be, all who had a taste similar to his own.

But, if the *opinions* of the heathens on this subject were false, no wonder that their *conduct* respecting it was wrong. If they mistook the nature of human happiness, they scarcely could succeed in the pursuit of it. If, placing it in *pleasure*, they sought it in the gratification of their appetites and passions, no wonder that, instead of the object they expected, they found remorse, disease, and death.

If in the *investigation of speculative truth,* no wonder they were at length convinced, as *Solomon* had been before them, that, in "much of such wisdom is much grief, and that he, who increaseth knowledge, increaseth sorrow." If they sought it in *riches* and *honours,* no wonder that care and vexation of heart were their reward. And, if they pursued even *virtue* herself, with the expectation of being perfectly happy in this life, no wonder they were sometimes disappointed; no wonder, while they thus mistook the object, to which she was conducting them, that she often appeared to them as a treacherous guide, or an empty name*.

This

---

* "O virtue!" exclaimed even *Brutus*, when oppressed by adverse fortune, "I have followed thee as a substantial good, but I find thou art an empty name."

This fruitful source of erroneous conduct the Gospel of Christ has removed. It teaches us, as I have already observed*, that the *greatest good*, to which man can aspire, is a sense of the approbation of his Maker; that this, in every stage of his existence, must be the foundation of his happiness, and the only unchangeable part of it; that all externals, respecting either the mind or the body, are of a relative nature, and affect him with pleasure or pain in a degree, which depends on his own disposition; that this disposition, at least during the present life, is always capable of improvement, and that therefore his happiness admits of an infinite variety of degrees; that the obstacles to it, which now so much abound, though adapted to his present state, are of an accidental and temporary nature, and will be removed in a future existence;

and

---

* Chap. II.

and, lastly, that enjoying, by a conformity between external objects and his inward disposition, the highest felicity, of which his nature, improved to what degree it may, shall be susceptible, he will continue to enjoy it for ever.

Such being the nature of the motives to virtue, with which the Christian revelation supplies us, I cannot but think the morality, which neglects the consideration of them, as extremely imperfect. There is, indeed, no rational pretence for doing so. If it be said, that future rewards are matters of *faith*, and not of *knowledge*, the same may, with equal truth, and with greater propriety of application, be said of the *present* rewards of virtue, as to their following in any particular case; for these, notwithstanding the natural tendency of things to confer them, are

often

often intercepted or diverted. In either cafe, however, this circumſtance ought not to be urged as an objection. Reaſons have already been ſuggeſted, why morality in general is matter of *probability*, rather than of ſtrict *demonſtration**; and theſe

---

* Chap. III. It may here be added, with reſpect to *motives* in particular, whether temporal or eternal, whether in the form of rewards, or in that of puniſhments, that, from the nature of motives, there is an obvious reaſon why, ſuppoſing them certain in themſelves, we cannot with certainty calculate their effect. A motive, which is irreſiſtible to one man, is not ſo to another; and, though there may be a limit, beyond which no man, poſſeſſed of common underſtanding, can reſiſt, yet freedom of action neceſſarily ſuppoſes, that every man has the power of reſiſting in ſome degree. What that degree is, in any particular perſon, will depend partly on his original conſtitution, and partly on the habits he may have contracted; ſo that different men will oppoſe a very different degree of reſiſtance to the ſame motive; and it is phyſically impoſſible to calculate before-hand the actual general effect of any particular one, even if we could diſtinctly ſtate what *ought* to be ſo.

Dr. *Paley*, on the ſubject of motives drawn from the ſuppoſition of moral inſtincts, ſays, "The remorſe ariſing from acting in oppoſition to them, may be borne with; and,
if

these reasons apply to the *motives*, as well as to the *rules* of virtue; and equally apply to them, whether discovered by the *light of nature*, or made known by *revelation*.

if the sinner choose to bear with it, for the sake of the immediate pleasure, or profit, &c. the moral instinct man, so far as I can understand, has nothing more to offer." However true this may be in fact, and however it may operate against the *sufficiency* of such motives, it ought to have no weight as an argument against either their existence or utility. Dr. *Paley* himself, indeed, does not employ it as an argument against their *existence*. Objections, the same in *kind*, though not the same in *degree*, may be made against *all* moral motives whatever. The sinner may, if he pleases, choose to run the hazard of *eternal* misery; and then, what has *any* moralist to say? Besides, moral instincts might exist as the *guide* to virtue, however little force they might have as the *motive*.

CHAP. V.

ON THE *DIVISION* OF VIRTUE.

THE *subject* of human virtue, or that, about which virtue is employed, may, I think, justly be considered as extending to *all the actions of men*. For, though all actions, in every state of circumstances, are not virtues or vices, the far greater part being, in fact, neither the one nor the other; yet circumstances may be supposed, in which all would become so. *Actions*, in the extensive sense, in which I have hitherto used the word, comprehend *thoughts*, the invisible actions of the mind; *words*, the audible expressions of them; and those visible and effective expressions of them, which are more usually and strictly called *actions*.

There

There is no need of any formal proof, that *words* and *actions* admit of moral qualities, or are capable of being virtuous or vicious. This will scarcely be disputed. With respect to *thoughts*, it may be proper to observe, that, since to God, whose will is the law of virtue, our thoughts are no less known than our words and actions, they must be equally the subject of virtue. It would be to no purpose for a man to be obedient to the will of God in his words and actions, if, in the inward frame of his mind, he were rebellious to it. If, as I have endeavoured to show, it be the object of moral discipline to improve the disposition of the mind, in order to its happiness, it will evidently follow, not only that the due regulation of the thoughts is a part of virtue, but that it is the most important part. External actions, as they affect the present happiness both

of

of the agent and of others, as they are declaratory of the difpofition of the mind, and as they tend to its improvement, are doubtlefs of great importance; but, if I miftake not, *thoughts*, as fpeaking the very language of the mind, and forming the effence of its difpofition, are ftill more important, and, in the eftimation of God, are all in all. If the idea of virtue did not extend to thoughts, many of the duties, which are owing more immediately to God and to ourfelves, and fome even of thofe, which are owing to our neighbour, would be excluded from the lift of virtues. Yet who can doubt, that much virtue may confift in having grateful thoughts of God for his goodnefs, and reverential thoughts of all his perfections? Who can doubt, that men may be virtuous in a careful regulation of their affections towards objects, according as

they

they are more likely to improve them in virtue?* Who can doubt, that it is virtuous to cherish grateful sentiments towards those, who have done us any kindness, even though we have no opportunity of expressing them? to respect and esteem the great and good, even though our respect and esteem can never affect them?

In the 4th Chapter, in order to give a clear idea of motives, I observed, that the mere

---

* I have before said, and shall soon have occasion to repeat it, that the *desire* of any thing, abstractedly from the circumstances, under which it is desired, does not constitute virtue or vice; and that the *regulation* of our affections towards objects, according as they are adapted to promote our happiness, is matter of *prudence* rather than of *virtue*. It does not hence follow, however, that the regulation of the affections may not be a part of virtue. When, with a view to our improvement in virtue, we "set our affection on things above, not on things on the earth," because a regard to the former is more likely to promote our improvement in it, we perform an act of virtue. In general, any act of the mind, which is performed on the principle of obeying God, is an act of virtue.

mere defire of any real or imaginary good, independently of all confideration of the manner, in which the gratification of it may be obtained, is not capable of being wrong. In the courfe of the fame Chapter, I have endeavoured, in dwelling on the neceffity of placing the affections on fuch objects, as are moft likely to be obtained by virtuous means, and moft adapted to promote our progrefs in virtue, to guard that obfervation againft the danger of misinterpretation. As a ftill further fecurity, it may be proper here to ftate more particularly the nature of the circumftances, on which the moral quality of the thoughts depends. Generally fpeaking, the defire of any thing under circumftances, in which we know or believe the poffeffion of it is *forbidden* by the law or will of God, is a vice of the thoughts, and the overcoming of the defire

fire is a virtue. It is when the objects of desire are invested with *circumstances*, that the desire of them becomes virtuous or vicious, and that they form the moral discipline of man*. The desirable nature of a thing forbidden constitutes *temptation*; but temptation is not *sin*. Were there no temptation, that is, were there no desirable things forbidden, there would, with respect to them, be neither virtue nor vice; no virtue in overcoming the desire of them, no vice in submitting to it. But, since it is the intention of the present state, to discipline us by the practice of virtue, it is wisely ordained, that almost every thing we meet with should be an exercise of virtue. In the case of *Adam*,

---

* This may be extended to *actions*. The putting a man to death, is sometimes *murder*, sometimes (in a *moral* sense) a matter of *indifference*, sometimes a *meritorious* action. The difference, in the several cases, arises from the difference of *circumstances*.

Adam, it was the *prohibition* to "eat of the tree of the knowledge of good and evil," which made it a sin in him to eat of it. Without the prohibition, there would have been no more harm in eating of that, than of any other tree in the garden. We may even conceive, that, before the prohibition was given, he did innocently eat of it. What constituted the sin of *Adam* was, not his looking upon the tree as desirable in itself, but as desirable under the circumstance of its being forbidden. We are accustomed to think, and not without reason, that there could not be a greater sin, than the eating of the forbidden fruit; and yet we see, that the sinfulness of the action entirely arose from the *circumstances*, under which it was performed; that the action itself, independently of the expression of God's will respecting it, was altogether indifferent;

indifferent; and that, consequently, the essence of the offence consisted in disobeying the will of God*.

In the peculiar situation of *Adam*, there was a necessity, in order to give room for the exercise of virtue, for a *positive* injunction. Without it, he had no opportunity of knowing the will of God concerning his actions. In a state of society, where we are able to collect the will of God concerning our actions from the probable effects of them, the case is different in this particular; but it is equally true, in every situation, that the criminality

---

* To those, who admit the authority of Scripture, this will seem an additional confirmation, if not of itself a proof, of my position, that *virtue consists in voluntary obedience to the will of God*.

In the fall of *Adam*, we see the probable fate of every undisciplined human being, and the necessity of those repeated acts of obedience to the divine will, by which alone a *habit* of obedience to it can be formed.

criminality of a desire arises, not from any thing in the nature of the desire itself, but from the circumstance, that it is forbidden by the will of God. Thus, in the instance of inordinate ambition formerly mentioned, as soon as the perception arises, that the desire is inconsistent with the will of God, it becomes morally wrong. We may know, from the attributes of God, discoverable from the works of creation and providence, that to obtain dominion over others in any way, which does not promote, or is not likely to promote, their good, cannot be agreeable to his will; and we may easily collect, from history and experience, that dominion over so considerable a portion of mankind is not to be obtained, without greatly interfering with their good.

A similar observation may be made,
with

with respect to the prohibition contained in the *tenth commandment*. The sin of coveting lies, not in the simple desire of the things there expressed and referred to; but in the desire of them notwithstanding their being our *neighbour's*.*

That much vice is exercised in the *thoughts*, without any external action, and in the *thoughts* and *words*, without any further external action, we may most clearly learn from our Saviour's interpretation of the sixth and seventh commandments†; and we may conclude, by

parity

---

* The *desire* of those things, therefore, of which the possession or enjoyment is forbidden by the law or will of God, is sinful. There is, however, this difference between a sin of the *thoughts* and a sin of *external action*, that the evil of the one is less extensive than the evil of the other. The ill effects of an offence of the *thoughts* are confined to him, who is guilty of it, and may, by the use of proper measures and due exertion, be in time corrected; whereas the mischief of a criminal *action* may affect others, and may be of such nature and extent, as not to admit of reparation.

† See *Matthew* v. 21—29.

parity of reason, that much virtue is exercised in the same manner*. It is evident, indeed, from the nature of the thoughts themselves, as forming the disposition of the mind, independently of their influence on our practice, that moralists can scarcely insist too much on the necessity of a due regulation of them, or take too much care to

" Guard the first spring of thought and will."

The distinguished superiority of the Christian over the heathen morality in this respect, and in giving those directions concerning the regulation of our affections, which are so necessary to be observed, in order to secure the practice of virtue, has been already noticed †; and to those, who

---

* It is mentioned as the great aggravation of the wickedness of the antediluvian world, that "every imagination of the thoughts of man's heart (his purposes and desires) was only evil continually."

† Chap. III.

who are desirous of obtaining a more complete idea of it, I repeat my recommendation of Dr. *Paley*'s animated Chapter on the subject, in his *View of the Evidences of Christianity*.

It may seem to some, that all this does not stand in need of much proof. It is a fact, however, that many systems of morality are deficient with respect to those duties, and those transgressions of duties, which are confined to the *thoughts*, and which do not manifest themselves in *words* or *actions*. Indeed, some of the ideas, which have been given of virtue, are such, that it would be difficult to show from them, that the regulation of the thoughts is any otherwise obligatory upon us, than as it is a *security* for virtuous practice. But, let us return to the more immediate subject of this Chapter.

The

The ancient division of virtue into the four cardinal ones of prudence, fortitude, temperance, and justice, is now very deservedly neglected. It neither comprehends all our duties, nor opens the way for a judicious distribution of those, which it does comprehend. Prudence, as I have already observed, is, strictly speaking, no part of virtue at all; but rather that branch of *wisdom*, by which we are directed, in any particular case, to take the measures necessary for our advantage*. Temperance and fortitude, as comprising a right behaviour both in prosperity and in adversity, may tolerably well express our duty to ourselves; but *justice*, though it denotes all the duties to our neighbour, which consist in not doing him any harm,

cannot

---

* If the idea of *prudence*, as explained by *Cicero* in his *Offices* (see L. I. C. 6.) be examined, it will not be found to contain in it any thing of the nature of virtue.

cannot with much propriety be extended to those, which consist in doing him good. *Cicero*, indeed, makes justice, or the head, which corresponds to it, to consist of two parts, namely, justice and beneficence; but this, surely, is giving up the original division. With respect to the duties, which we owe immediately to God, they seem either to be entirely omitted in this division, or to be placed, if ranked under the head of justice, in a subordinate point of view, as tending merely to preserve the good order of society. This at least is the light, in which they are considered, slightly as they are considered, by *Cicero*; for he defines the whole head of *justice* to be "ea ratio, quâ societas hominum inter ipsos, et vitæ quasi communitas continetur." Indeed, the notion, which *Cicero* had adopted concerning the Gods, or on which at least he proceeded in his

Offices,

Offices, as if it were not consistent with their nature to inflict *punishment*,* put it out of his power to enter into this class of duties with much effect; and we may say in general, respecting this division of virtue, that, if it ever was a good one, it was much better suited to *heathen* than to *Christian* morality.

The division of duties, whether of thought, word, or action, with a respect to those, who may be the immediate *objects* of them, that is, God, our neighbour, and ourselves, seems to be the most convenient; and it has the recommendation of being countenanced by Scripture, and by the offices of our national Church.

There

---

* "Sed, quia *Deos nocere non putant*, his exceptis, homines hominibus obesse plurimum arbitrantur." L. II. C. 3. "At hoc quidem commune est omnium philosophorum nunquam nec *irasci* Deum, nec *nocere*." L. III. C. 28.

There are, then, two divisions, under which the duties of morality seem naturally to fall; one referring to the manner, in which they are performed by the agent, as being *thoughts, words* or *actions*; the other to the immediate objects of them, as being duties to *God,* our *neighbour,* or *ourselves.* As each division is made up of three parts, we may, from a combination of both, obtain nine convenient heads, to which virtue may be reduced. To one or other of them all such human actions as, from the circumstances, under which they are performed, admit of moral qualities, may be referred. Were I, therefore, to compose a system of morality, I should class the duties thus:

FIRST CLASS*.

1. Duties of thought towards God.
2. Duties

---
* All these duties are, properly speaking, *moral* duties;
but,

2. Duties of word towards God.
3. Duties of action towards God.

SECOND CLASS.

1. Duties of thought towards our neighbour.
2. Duties of word towards our neighbour.
3. Duties of action towards our neighbour.

THIRD CLASS.

1. Duties of thought towards ourselves.
2. Duties of word towards ourselves.
3. Duties of action towards ourselves.

On the inaccuracy of Dr. *Paley's* definition of virtue, I may seem already to have sufficiently remarked. The subject of this Chapter, however, leads me further

but, as I have already observed, those of the first class may, by way of eminence, be called *religious* duties.

further to say respecting it, that, in confining virtue to *acts of beneficence*, he renders it incapable of either of these divisions. It follows, from Dr. *Paley*'s definition, as he himself observes, that " the subject of virtue is the *good of mankind*;" which, though it may be divided into *thoughts, words,* and *actions,* cannot easily be made to comprehend all virtuous thoughts, words, and actions, nor at all to admit of the division into duties towards *God,* our *neighbour,* and *ourselves.* Dr. *Paley,* it is true, in his explanation and proof of the several duties, does make use of the latter division; but he cannot, surely, be thought to have done so in strict consistence with his own definition. It is not easy to see how the *good of mankind,* though very well expressive of our duty towards our neighbour, can comprehend either

either our duty towards God, or our duty towards ourselves. There are many duties owing to God, which have no reference to our neighbour, and which we should be under an obligation to observe, were we alone on the earth; and, though there are some duties owing to ourselves, which have that reference, there are many, which are more confined, which would equally be duties in a state of solitude, and which it would be preposterous to say are owing to ourselves as being a *part* of mankind*. The truth is, that Dr. *Paley*, whether misled by his definition or not, has not treated of either of these classes of

---

* It is easy to suppose, without having recourse to the unauthenticated case of *Robinson Crusoe*, that a person may be cut off from society, so as to have no reasonable hope of returning to it; and it is evident, that such an one would be under a moral obligation of observing a certain conduct towards himself, whether the love of life, or any other consideration, proved a sufficient inducement to his observance of it or not.

of duties so fully, as might be wished and expected. The last in particular, though a copious subject for the moralist, is dispatched in three short Chapters; whereas, in the MS heads of Lectures, from which the late Dr. *Balguy* some years since gave a course of Lectures in morality to the Students of St. *John*'s College, in *Cambridge*, and from which the following is a transcript, there are no less than eighteen heads of duties owing to ourselves, each of which, as the reader will easily perceive, admits of much useful explanation.

" Of actions considered as beneficial or hurtful to the agent.

1. General principle.
2. Of the due care of our persons; and, first, the duty of preserving our own lives, and the crime of suicide.

3. Of the preservation and recovery of health.

4. Of the improvement and preservation of the several faculties of the body and mind.

5. The duty of temperance explained from the two preceding articles.

6. Of undue or excessive care of our persons.

7. The duty of fortitude, and the opposite vices of effeminacy and cowardice explained from the preceding article.

8. Of the due care of our fortunes; and, first, of industry in *acquiring* wealth.

9. Of frugality in *using* it.

10. Of undue or excessive care of our fortune.

11. The vice of avarice explained from the preceding article.

12. Of the due care of our reputation.

13. Of undue or exceſſive care of it.

14. The terms modeſty and vanity explained from the preceding articles.

15. Of caution in avoiding the enmity and ill offices of other men.

16. Of aſſiduity in ſeeking their friendſhip and good offices.

17. The means to be uſed for avoiding the one, and obtaining the other.

18. The reaſon, why the cultivation of the underſtanding, and the regulation of the paſſions are not conſidered more particularly in this Chapter*."

It

---

* The Lectures delivered from the Syllabus, from which this is a tranſcript, form another work of Dr. *Balguy's*, with which, I hope, at ſome time or other, the public will be favoured. Dr. *Hey*, the late Norriſian Profeſſor, read Lectures at *Sidney* College from the ſame Syllabus. Some of theſe I had the pleaſure and the profit of hearing; and I am not ſingular in the wiſh, that theſe alſo may be publiſhed; and that Students may enjoy the advantage of the

It may further be remarked, respecting this part of Dr. *Paley's* definition of virtue, that, if he is right in considering a regard to the *utility* of any action, as expressive of the *will of God* concerning it, as he does B. II. C. 4. it will follow, that the "doing good to mankind" is virtually expressed in the term "obedience to the will of God;" and, consequently, that it cannot be *expressed* in the definition without some degree of tautology. The conclusion,

the same candid and diligent investigation with respect to *Morality*, which by the publication of Dr. *Hey's* Norrisian Lectures, they enjoy with respect to *Divinity*.

Since writing the above, I have had the satisfaction of learning, that the MSS of Dr. *Balguy*, relating to *Morality*, have been put into the hands of Dr. *Hey*. There is no room to doubt, therefore, that, in due time, they will be given to the world in the form, which is adapted to render them of most use. With respect to his MSS on the subject of *Natural Religion*, of which, as I have noticed, "Divine Benevolence asserted," was published as a specimen, I add, with regret, that I understand them not to be in such a state, as encourages much hope of our seeing the "outlines," drawn in the Advertisement to that masterly work, "filled up."

conclusion, which I draw from this, is, that, even according to Dr. *Paley's* principles, virtue is, simply, " obedience (voluntary obedience) to the will of God."

In order to illustrate the distribution, which I have proposed, I will give a specimen of the duties, which are comprehended under each head. The corresponding transgression of each duty will suggest itself of course, and need not be particularly mentioned*. To aim at

a

---

* The reader will have observed, that, according to *my* moral vocabulary, the terms *sinful, criminal, vicious,* since they all denote offences against the will of God, are nearly synonymous. I have, however, no objection, for the sake of distinction, to consider *sins* as breaches of duties owing more immediately to God, *crimes* as breaches of duties owing to our neighbours, and *vices* as breaches of duties owing to ourselves. This agrees pretty well, but not exactly, with the distinction observed by Mr. *Locke,* who (Essay, B. II. C. 28.) says, that " divine law is the measure of *sin* and *duty*; civil law the measure of *crimes* and *innocence*; philosophic law, or the law of opinion and reputation, the measure of *virtue* and *vice.*"

a complete enumeration of duties, to describe any of them particularly, to prove the obligation to observe them, or to alledge the motives to their observance, all of which would be necessary in a *system* of morality, does not come within the design of these Remarks.

DUTIES of the FIRST CLASS*.

FIRST HEAD.

Reverential thoughts of God's perfections.

Grateful thoughts of God's mercies and favours.

Love of God.

Fear

---

* It is to be observed in general of this table, and indeed of any more complete one of the same kind, that it is nothing more than an enumeration of actions, which are agreeable to the will of God. In order to render them instances of *virtue*, it is necessary, that they be performed under the idea of their *being* agreeable to the will of God. The mere *performance* of them is not sufficient for this purpose.

Fear of God.

Truſt in God.

Humble thoughts of our unworthineſs in the ſight of God.

Convictions, that we obtain ſalvation only by means of the covenant eſtabliſhed through the merits of *Chriſt*; and that we are enabled to perform the conditions of that covenant only by the aſſiſtance of the *Holy Spirit*.

Duties of thought, reſulting from theſe convictions, towards the *Firſt Perſon* of the Holy Trinity.

------towards the *Second Perſon*.

------towards the *Third Perſon*.

Mental prayer.

SECOND HEAD.

Private vocal prayer.

Abſtinence from vain oaths, and every irreverent uſe of God's name.

Religious conversation.

THIRD HEAD.

Family prayer.
Public prayer*.
Observance of the sabbath †.

Observance

---

* It may happen, that a duty, taken in its most extensive sense, is not confined to one head of the class, to which it belongs. Thus, mental prayer may be considered as a duty of the first head; private vocal prayer as a duty of the first and second; public prayer as a duty of the first, second, and third; i. e. as a duty of *thought*, *word*, and *action*. This may sometimes render it doubtful to which head a particular duty belongs. It seems most proper, however, to refer it to the second, if it comprehend the first and the second, and to the third, if it comprehend them all.

† According to the common phraseology, which distinguishes *moral* duties from *positive*, it may seem, that positive duties cannot properly be admitted into a system of *morality*. I have, however, suggested reasons, which to me appear satisfactory, for calling all the duties, which we owe to God, our neighbour, or ourselves, *moral* duties, whatever may be the means, by which we discover them to be duties. We are under a moral obligation to the observance of every thing, which we know or believe to be agreeable to the will of God, whether the grounds, on which our knowledge

or

Observance of the Christian sacraments. Attentions towards persons and things appropriated to divine worship, whether by personal services, pecuniary contributions, or otherwise.

DUTIES or belief is founded, be natural or revealed. When moral and positive duties are opposed to each other merely for the sake of pointing out the different methods, by which we arrive at the knowledge of them, no great harm can arise from it. In any other view, it tends to encourage the idea, even in cases where no *interference* is supposed, that the one class of duties is less obligatory than the other. Were it not, therefore, for the inconvenience, which attends a change of terms, I should propose to call the one *rational* or *natural*, and the other *revealed* duties; as being denominations less liable to misinterpretation, and better adapted to point out the distinction intended. The command to *Adam*, to forbear eating of a particular fruit, was a *revealed* duty; yet none, who admit the truth of revelation, will deny, that he was under a *moral* obligation to observe it.

Though this is not the place for *practical* remarks, I cannot let pass this last occasion of mentioning the observance of the Sabbath as a moral duty, without reminding the reader how incumbent it is on those, who would pay a due regard to moral obligations, to encourage no mode of spending the Sabbath, which may lead to the breach of such an obligation. As masters of families, we ought not, on

that

DUTIES of the SECOND CLASS.

FIRST HEAD.

Love of mankind.

Respect and esteem for the great and good.

that day, to exercise, to demand, or to permit works of either business or pleasure, which may hinder ourselves or others from what, under the Christian dispensation, is to be considered as the essential part of the observance of the Sabbath, the *public worship of God*. Without Jewish superstition, or Puritanical preciseness, let us contribute our endeavours to make the Sabbath, agreeably to the meaning of the term, so far a day of *rest*, as to afford an opportunity to those, who would not otherwise enjoy it, of performing religious services, and receiving religious instruction. An attempt was lately made, honourable to the individuals, who made it, to check the profanation of the Sabbath, by the prohibition, under heavier penalties than at present, of Sunday Newspapers. If success in that attempt had at all promised to render the observance of Sunday more like what it ought to be, I should have looked forward to it with great satisfaction. But I cannot help thinking, that nothing will effectually be done to this purpose, until those, whose conduct is the object of imitation, and who must therefore greatly influence the conduct of others, shall bring themselves to set a better example. When a rich or fashionable man breaks the Sabbath, he probably occasions fifty others

Sorrow for the sins and calamities of men.

Wishes for their improvement and happiness.

Guarding against immoderate anger, resentment, contempt, envy, &c.

Favourable judgment in doubtful cases.

to break it with him. How is it, that persons in the higher ranks of life, who have so much better opportunities than others of being informed of their duty, and who, in this instance, have so much fewer temptations to transgress it, are so openly unmindful of it? If any ranks of people have an excuse for making Sunday a day of mere relaxation and amusement, certainly the lower ranks, who, on other days, are under an obligation of labour and confinement, can plead it with most reason. What would a Gentleman *say*, if, on driving into an Inn-yard on a Sunday, he were told, that the ostlers and postilions were gone to church? What ought he to *think* and *feel*, if he were conscious, that they remained at home, in expectation of his coming? Certain it is, that, while the *custom* of travelling on Sundays continues so prevalent, the detention from church of a great part of the family at every posting Inn will continue also; and whoever, by his practice, contributes to support the custom, is answerable, in some degree, for all its consequences.

SECOND

SECOND HEAD.

Abstinence from false testimony against others.

Abstinence from injurious or provoking appellations.

Abstinence from slander, detraction, &c.

Giving good advice.

Promoting useful conversation.

THIRD HEAD.

Abstinence from actions injurious to others, whether in their persons or possessions.

Particulars comprehended under the last article.

Rendering honour to parents.

Obedience to civil governors.

Respectful behaviour to superiors.

Condescension to inferiors.

Protection of dependents.

Gentleness

Gentleness and beneficence to all men.

DUTIES of the THIRD CLASS.

FIRST HEAD.

Regulation of the passions and affections, with a view to improvement in virtue.

Humility.

Resignation.

Contentment.

Fortitude.

Courage*.

SECOND

---

* Though these terms may be thought to denote certain dispositions of the mind, rather than particular acts of virtue, they properly enough come under the notion of *duties*; because, in whatever state such dispositions may be, they are always capable of improvement by suitable acts of the mind; and because, under the name of each particular disposition, are comprehended the acts of the mind, by which it is improved.

SECOND HEAD.

Since the faculty of speech can be employed, at least with any meaning, only in communicating ideas to *others*, it may seem, that no duties, which depend on a right use of it, can exclusively affect ourselves; and that, therefore, there are no duties belonging to this head. There are, however, various abuses of the faculty of speech, not injurious to others, which yet are inconsistent with the reverence due to ourselves; such as the want of veracity in things indifferent, vain boasting, indulgence in idle and unprofitable talk; and the instances, in which these abuses are avoided on *principle*, are so many duties observed towards ourselves.

THIRD

SIXTH CLASS.

Preservation of life and health, by temperance, exercise, the avoiding of unnecessary dangers, &c.

Care of our reputation.

Industry.

Frugality.

Cultivation of our faculties.

CONCLUSION.

CONCLUSION.

HAVING gone distinctly through the different parts of the subject, I may now venture to give a concise statement of the whole; a statement, which, though it might have been rejected, if proposed at first, may now, perhaps, be admitted without much difficulty.

In the first Chapter, we have, I think, seen, that the sole *foundation* of human virtue is the will of God*; the will of

---

* That this is the foundation of virtue to a *religious* man, all will readily admit; and there is, as I have said, a *primâ facie* presumption, that the virtue of a religious man is of the same nature with that of every other man; a religious man differing from others, who have any just pretensions to virtue, not in acting on a different principle, or from different motives, but in paying peculiar attention to that class of moral duties, which are owing more immediately to God, or which have God for their immediate object.

of that Being, who is the creator and continual preserver of men, and who, in their creation and preservation, must necessarily be supposed to design their observance of the conduct, which is best adapted to answer the end of their creation and preservation, and which, therefore, as created and dependent beings it is their *duty* to observe*. We have also seen, in the second Chapter, that the particulars of this conduct are not reducible to any *one* declaration or expression of the will of God, as an *universal*

---

* It hence follows, that all morality is necessarily built on *religion*: for it is by the knowledge of God's nature and attributes, with which religion furnishes us, that we make deductions respecting what his will in particular cases is. It hence also follows, that no one can separate virtue from religion, or with any propriety say, 'As to *religion*, I make no pretension to it; but I think myself bound to be *virtuous.*' For, if religion be understood to mean the knowledge of God's will, it is evident, that virtue implies a constant regard to it. If it mean the performance of *religious duties*, it is, as has been shown, no other than a *part* of virtue itself.

verſal rule of virtue; but that they are to be collected from all the declarations or expreſſions of his will, of which different men, according to their different capacities and ſituations, have the opportunity of obtaining the knowledge; that, though general rules of conduct may be uſeful, yet no rule is ſo general, as to be applicable to all caſes; and that (as, for various reaſons, was to be expected) much, in every caſe, is left to the judgment and diſcretion of the particular agent*. It is alſo noticed, as a neceſſary reſult of the
leading

---

* Thus, the right conduct in particular inſtances, with reſpect to promiſes made to robbers, madmen, &c. cannot be deduced from any general rule; but muſt be determined, by the judgment of the promiſer, from the circumſtances of the caſe. In fact, to perſons acting in theſe and ſimilar ſituations, different moraliſts, led or miſled by an adherence to their reſpective rules, often preſcribe different modes of conduct. My oppoſition, however, to ſuch rules of virtue, as thoſe laid down by Dr. *Clarke*, Mr. *Wollaſton*, Dr. *Paley*, &c. conſiſts, as I have ſaid, not in refuſing to admit them as rules, but as *univerſal* and *excluſive* rules.

leading principle, that, since virtue depends not on mere conformity to the *rule* of virtue, or on the external effect of actions, the conduct, which looks not beyond these, which has no reference, immediate or mediate, to the will of God, however conformable it may be to any *rule* of virtue, and however beneficial to the world or to the agent, is not *virtuous* conduct. In the third Chapter, in order to preclude any idea, which might arise from what had been stated, of our being at liberty to act as we please, so long as we act according to our knowledge, I have endeavoured to show, that there is the same obligation on us to obtain the knowledge of the will of God, as there is to perform his will when known; and that, therefore, we are under obligation to employ, for that purpose, all the methods in our power,

whether

whether of *reason* or of *revelation*. In the fourth Chapter, I have stated it as my opinion, that the motives to action in general are founded in *self-love*, and have regard to our own happiness; and that, therefore, it is no objection to a scheme of morality, that its motives are reducible to that passion. In proof of this, I have observed, that, in determining the moral quality of actions, we ought to distinguish between *motive* and *principle*; and, having endeavoured to show, that virtue depends altogether on *principle*, I have thence concluded, that it is not essential to virtue, that the motive to it should be of any particular *kind*; that, though one motive may be more favourable than another to the practice of virtue, yet that, wherever voluntary obedience to the will of God exists, there virtue exists, whatever may be the motive, by which the agent

is

is actuated; and that, on the contrary, there is no virtue in the endeavour to obtain or avoid any object, unlefs we are directed, in the endeavour to obtain or avoid it, by the principle of fuppofed obedience to the will of God. It hence follows, that though, in human beings, conftituted as they are, it be in vain to look for the actual exertions of virtue, without a reference to motives, without a regard to incitements, which are founded in felf-love, yet virtue is, in itfelf, altogether independent of motives; is not more or lefs fo by any change of motives; and that, confequently, though many actions, beneficial to the agent and to the world, may arife folely from motives, from an exclufive regard to the object, which the agent has in view*, they then only become

virtues,

---

* That is, when the principle of action either coincides with the motive, or is fuperfeded by it.

virtues, when they are performed on the principle of obedience to the divine will. As, in the third Chapter, I had referred to the obligation, under which we ſtand to revelation, and particularly to the Chriſtian revelation, for teaching us what our duty is; ſo, in this, I referred to the no leſs important obligation we owe to it, for ſupplying us with thoſe motives, by which we are induced to perform our duty, more eſpecially the promiſe of eternal happineſs on the one hand, and the threat of eternal miſery on the other; thence deducing the concluſion, that Chriſtianity is juſtly to be conſidered as a moſt powerful inſtrument in the furtherance of virtue. In the fifth and laſt Chapter, I have propoſed, as matter of convenience, a diviſion of the *ſubject* of virtue into duties of thought, word, and deed, towards God, our neighbour, and
ourſelves;

ourselves; making nine heads, to one or other of which all human actions, admitting of moral qualities, may be referred.

All the particulars, which are here enumerated, have, I believe, by some moralists or other, and in some way or other, been admitted into their systems. It has generally happened, however, that those, who admitted one, have been over-suspicious respecting the rest. Those, who considered the will of God as the foundation of morality, have been afraid of admitting such rules of virtue, as are laid down by Dr. *Clarke*, Mr. *Wollaston*, Dr. *Paley*, &c. and still more so of admitting any regard to self-advantage, especially if that advantage was of a temporal nature; whereas, when the one are considered as mere *expressions* of the will of God, and the other as the *motive*

to

to its observance, they do not at all interfere with it as the *foundation*. Those, who considered any thing else than the will of God as the foundation of morality, and particularly those, who considered *self-love* as that foundation, have, so far as they preserved a consistency with themselves, necessarily rejected all effectual reference to the will of God, and confounded either the *principle* of virtue with the *rule*, or both principle and rule with the *motive*.

The *peculiarity*, therefore, of what I have attempted, consists in this, that, whereas others have admitted into their systems of morality, whether as the *foundation*, the *rule*, or the *motive* of virtue, obedience to the will of God, conformity to truth, conformity to the eternal fitness of things, the moral sense, regard to the

good

good of mankind, regard to private happiness, &c. but have admitted one or more of these particulars *separately*, always to the disparagement, and generally to the exclusion, of any other, I have endeavoured to show, that there is not such an incompatability between them, as has been supposed; that the admission of some does not necessarily imply the exclusion of the rest; but that, when they have their proper place in the subject, they are all perfectly consistent with each other, and contribute their parts towards the formation of one harmonious whole.

FINIS.

www.ingramcontent.com/pod-product-compliance
Lightning Source LLC
Chambersburg PA
CBHW081325090426

42737CB00017B/3035